Why Kindergarten Matters

Also from Westphalia Press

Why Kindergarten Matters

Elizabeth Harrison's
A Study Of Child-Nature

Edited and introduced by
Paul Rich

WESTPHALIA PRESS
An imprint of Policy Studies Organization

Why Kindergarten Matters
Elizabeth Harrison's
A Study of Child-Nature

Westphalia Press
An imprint of Policy Studies Organization
dgutierrezs@ipsonet.org

For information:
Westphalia Press
1527 New Hampshire Ave., N.W.
Washington, D.C. 20036

ISBN-13: 978-1935907275
ISBN-10: 1935907271

Updated material and comments on this edition can
be found at the Westphalia Press website:
westphaliapress.org

This edition is dedicated to
Nivine Megahed, President of National Louis
University and Innovator in the Tradition of
Elizabeth Harrison

INTRODUCTION TO THIS NEW EDITION

Elizabeth Harrison and National Louis University

Elizabeth Harrison was a pioneer in early childhood education who in 1886 established what is now National Louis University in Chicago. She is rightly considered a founder of the American kindergarten movement and of the Parent Teacher Association. At the time, she was thought radical in her belief that teaching was a profession that needed college credentials and that early education deserved status and resources.

The Chicago Kindergarten College established itself on Michigan Avenue in 1906 and began its progress to being a major university. In 1986 what was then the National College of Education received a thirty million dollar gift from the civic leader Michael W. Louis and soon after the university was named National Louis

University, to commemorate the many acts of service through the years of the Louis family.

While other campuses of National Louis ring Chicago and are located in Florida and Wisconsin, it continues as an important part of the city's life with alumni in significant positions in education, government and business. Elizabeth Harrison had an unshakable belief in what education could do for society, as the following pages make clear, and she would not be disappointed that what she started has continued and prospered.

Paul Rich
Garfield House, Washington DC

F

A

STUDY OF CHILD-NATURE

FROM

THE KINDERGARTEN STANDPOINT

BY

ELIZABETH HARRISON

PRINCIPAL OF THE CHICAGO KINDERGARTEN COLLEGE

EIGHTEENTH EDITION

PUBLISHED BY
THE CHICAGO KINDERGARTEN COLLEGE
10 Van Buren St.
1898

PREFACE.

These Talks for Mothers and Teachers were given before my classes in Chicago and elsewhere. They are now published at the earnest request of the members of those classes, and are in nearly the same form as when given, which accounts for the number of anecdotes illustrating different points, as well as for the frequency of personal reminiscence. Fully aware of their many defects, but knowing well that "Charity covereth a multitude of sins," I give them with a loving heart to the mothers of America. I hope that the thought underlying them may be as helpful to others in the understanding of little children as it has been to me. I trust that these pages may lead each reader to a deeper study of Froebel's thought.

E. H.

CONTENTS.

INTRODUCTION.

In the educational world is growing the realization, in a practical way, that "The hand that rocks the cradle rules the world." The importance of the first years of the child's life is beginning to be acknowledged; his physical welfare has become a recognized study, for it is seen that the health and strength of maturity depends upon this early growth. Until the time of Froebel, the founder of the Kindergarten system, scarcely any thought was given to the right or wrong training of the infant's natural instincts; few people dreamed that this had aught to do with the development of character in succeeding years.

The child's manifestations of these inborn instincts have been laughed at, played with, and even related as interesting anecdotes by the fond mother,—the thought that they are worthy of serious study seldom entering the mind of the average parent. It is this study to which Froebel invites the mother. He calls it "The Science of Motherhood."

Investigation of apparently insignificant instincts shows them to be the germs of world-wide and ever-enduring truths. Hence the importance of the Kindergarten study. The mother is aided by it in the care and understanding of her young child when the bond between them is so strong that instinct is apt to give the right impulse; she is also greatly assisted in the comprehension of her child's more mature years, after the growth of his individuality has somewhat separated them. "The child is father to the man" in character as well as in physical development. We readily acknowledge this when we admit that superstitions cling to the wisest minds,—such as a distaste for beginning a piece of work on Friday; an uneasy sensation when the salt-cellar is upset; a dislike to see the new moon over the left shoulder, and other irrational prejudices. When we remember that all one's after-life cannot entirely obliterate them, do we not realize how lasting are early impressions?

Froebel has said: "The destiny of the nations lies far more in the hands of women— the mothers—than in the hands of those who possess power, or those who are innovators, who seldom understand themselves. *We must cultivate women,* who are the educators of the human race, else a new generation cannot accomplish its task."

One of the greatest lines of the world's work lies here before us: the understanding of little children, in order that they may be properly trained. Correctly understood, it demands of women her highest endeavor, the broadest culture, the most complete command of herself, and the understanding of her resources and environments. It demands of her that she become a physician, an artist, a teacher, a poet, a philosopher, a priest. In return, it gives her an insight into science, into history, into art, into literature, into human nature, such as no other culture can command, because each of these realms has to be entered that its wealth may be conquered as an aid in rightly understanding the little child entrusted to her care, not for the added glory it will bring to her.

The following facts place this study of child-culture upon the broad basis of a science.

FIRST: THE CHILD BEARS WITHIN HIMSELF INSTINCTS WHICH CAN BE TRAINED UPWARD OR DOWNWARD.

SECOND: THESE INSTINCTS GIVE EARLY MANIFESTATION OF THEIR EXISTENCE.

THIRD: THE MOTHER'S LOVING GUIDANCE CAN BE CHANGED FROM UNCERTAIN INSTINCT INTO UNHESITATING INSIGHT.

Let me illustrate this change of instinct into insight. A young mother, who had been studying Froebel for some months, placed her four-year-old boy in my Kindergarten. I soon saw that he was suffering from self-consciousness. In a conversation with the mother, I told her that I had discovered in her child a serious obstacle to mental growth, viz., self-consciousness. "What is the cause of it?" said she. "If the child had not such a sensible mother," I replied, "I should say that he had been 'shown off' to visitors until the habit of thinking that every one is looking at him has become fixed in his mind." Instantly the blood mounted to her face and she said: "That is what has been done. You know that he sings very well; last winter my young sister frequently had him stand on a chair beside the piano and sing for guests. I *felt* at the time that it was not right, but if I had known then what I now do, I would have died rather than have allowed it."

Instinct is often overruled by others; *insight* makes the mother stand invincible for her child's right to be properly brought up.

CHAPTER I.

THE BODY.

THE INSTINCT OF ACTIVITY, OR THE TRAINING OF THE MUSCLES.

All little children are active; constant activity is nature's way of securing physical development. A seemingly superfluous amount of nervous force is generated in each growing child. The organs of respiration, circulation and digestion use their needful share. The rest of this nervous power is expended by the infant, in tossing his limbs about, in creeping and crawling; by the growing boy, in climbing and running; by the young girl—who must not climb or run, as such conduct is not ladylike—in twisting, squirming and giggling; thus gaining for her muscles, in spite of prohibition, some of the needed exercise. Making a restless child "keep still" is a repression of this nervous energy, which irritates the whole nervous system, causing ill-temper, moroseness and general uncomfortableness. If this force could be properly expended, the child would be always sunny-tempered. The mother's instinctive feeling that the restlessness of her child is necessary to its well-being, gives her strength to endure what would be unendurable confusion and noise to any one who has not this maternal instinct. But the wise mother who has changed this dim instinct into luminous insight, turns the riot into joyous, happy play or other wholesome activity. By this course not only does she lessen the strain upon her own nerves, but what is of more importance, often avoids a clash of will power between herself and her child; such clashing of wills being always fraught with harm to both.

In order that this activity, generally first noticed in the use of the hands, might be trained into right and ennobling habits rather than be allowed to degenerate into wrong and often degrading ones, Froebel arranged his charming set of finger games for the mother to teach her babe while he is yet in her arms; thus establishing the right activity before the wrong one can assert itself.

In such little songs as the following:

> " This is the mother, good and dear,
> This the father, with hearty cheer,
> This is the brother, stout and tall,

> This is the sister, who plays with her doll,
> And this is the baby, the pet of all.
> Behold the good family, great and small!"

the child is led to personify his fingers and to
regard them as a small but united family over
which he has control. Of course, this song
can be varied to suit the phase of family-life
with which he is surrounded. For instance:

> " This is the auntie, who wears a bright shawl,
> This is the brother, who plays with his ball,"

or like rhythmical descriptions. The little fingers may be put to sleep, one by one, with
some such words as these:

> " Go to sleep, little thumb, that's one,
> Go to sleep, pointing finger, two,
> Go to sleep, middle finger, three,
> Go to sleep, ring finger, four,
> Go to sleep, little finger, five.
> I take them and tuck them snugly all in bed, sound asleep.
> Let naught disturb them."

To the little fingers thus quietly closed
against the palm of the hand can be sung some
soft lullaby, and the quieting effect upon the
babe is magical.

Once while travelling upon a railway train,
I watched for a time the vain endeavors of a
young mother to persuade her restless boy of
two years to be undressed for bed. Finally I

went to the rescue, and began to talk to the little fellow about the queer finger family that lived on his hand. I gave him a name for each member of this family, and in a few minutes suggested that they were sleepy and that we had better put them to bed. He was delighted. Singing softly the ditty just mentioned, I showed him how to fold first one, then another of the chubby fingers in seeming sleep. When we had finished he was very still; the pleasing activity had called his thoughts away from his capricious, willful little self; he had something to do. "Now," said I, "do you think you can undress without waking these babies?" He nodded a pleased assent. The mother took him off and in a short time came back and thanked me, saying, that while he was being undressed his thoughts had been concentrated upon keeping his fingers undisturbed, and that he had dropped asleep with his hand tightly closed. She was astonished at this power of the game, yet the device was simple; the nervous, restless activity of the child was turned from a wrong channel into a right one. By many such means, Froebel would have the baby's fingers seem to him tiny people of whom he has charge.

When these games are emphasized with an older child who can *work* with his hands, there is danger of his separating, in thought, himself from his fingers, making them alone responsible for their deeds, and of his setting entirely aside his own obligation in the matter. For example: In my Kindergarten there was a boy who had a very bad habit with his hands, a fault not uncommon with children of all classes. At once I laid more stress upon the finger families and his care of them. After a day or two had passed, I noticed that he was not following directions in sewing his card. "Oh, dear!" I said, " how came these crooked lines here?"

"Well, those fingers, they did it. They don't care how they work," was his reply. I saw that I had brought out too much their individuality, and too little his accountability for them. "Ah," I answered, "but who has charge of this family? You must help the fingers take out these wrong stitches and show them how to put in the right ones."

To some these incidents may seem childish, yet underlying them is one of the world's greatest principles of development, viz: cultivate right tendencies in humanity and the wrong ones must die out. *Build up the posi-*

2

tive side of your child's nature and the nega-
tive side will not need to be unbuilt.

Let me illustrate more fully this important
thought. At the age of two or three years,
according to the immaturity or maturity of
the child, the instinct of investigation begins
to show itself, developing in various ways an
appalling power of destruction; such as tear-
ing to pieces his doll, smashing his toy-bank,
cutting holes in his apron, and many other indications of seeming depravity. It is a critical period. Without this important instinct,
man would have made but little progress in
civilization; it is the basis of scientific and
mathematical research, of study in all fields.
This legitimate and natural investigative activity needs only to be led from the negative
path of *destruction,* into the positive one of
construction. Instead of vainly attempting to
suppress the new-born power of the young
pioneer, or searcher after truth, guide it
aright. Give him playthings which can be
taken to pieces and put together again without
injury to the material; dolls which can be
dressed and undressed; horses which can be
harnessed and unharnessed; carts to which
horses may be fastened at will, or any like
toys. Blocks which can be built into various

new forms are admirable playthings for children; the more of their own ideas they can put into the re-arrangement, the better. It is the divine right of each human being to re-construct in his own way, *when that way does not interfere with the care of property, or the rights of others.* The glorious instinct of creativity —one of the best evidences that man is made in the image of God—also is cultivated.

Froebel's system of child-culture is based upon laws that are supported by the three-fold testimony of nature, history, and revelation. We see these positive and negative possibilities of which I have just been speaking, in all creation. In the physical world they appeal to our senses for recognition. Look at any wayside field with its luxuriant crop of weeds; one may plow and harrow, may prepare the soil with diligence, but unless the right kind of seeds are planted, the weeds will again have full possession. I was told by a leading physician in the Engadine Valley in Switzerland, who had made a life-time study of diseases of the lungs, that if a person inheriting consumptive tendencies were placed in the right climate, his constitution could so be built up that the dread tendency would die out, or remain dormant and not develop, even though the inheritance had been continuous through many generations. This statement was confirmed by a prominent London physician, and I believe is now the accepted theory.

The same principle is shown in the world of history, that our reason may assent to it. As we thoughtfully turn its pages, what is the record we find? Is it not as soon as a nation has arrived at a period when pioneer work ceases, when conquest over surrounding nature, or adjacent nations, is no longer a necessity, when wealth has brought leisure, that then, and not until then, self-indulging vice and destroying corruption creep in? The positive activity of the nation has ceased, and its negative activity at once begins.

With equal clearness is this proclaimed in the world of revelation that we may know it to be the truth of God. What lesson is taught in the Scripture parable of the man who drove out the devil, then swept and garnished his house and left it *empty*, when seven other demons came and dwelt therein?

This thought was well understood by the mother whose boy of fourteen was coming home alone for a summer vacation, a journey of a day and a half. Knowing that he had once before fallen into the habit of reading

bad books, and fearing that his will-power
was not yet strong enough to resist the temptation to read the trash sold upon the train,
she bought new copies of the " St. Nicholas"
and " Youths' Companion" and sent them to
him with the loving message that he would
probably wish something to read on the way.
When he reached home he began at once to
tell her of an article in the "St. Nicholas"
which had attracted him, and of a " boss
story" he had found in the " Youth's Companion." No thought had entered his mind
of buying other reading matter, nor had there
been any chafing sense of prohibition. The
success of our Young Men's Christian Associa-
tions is to be attributed to this same positive
upbuilding principle. When they wish to
close a saloon, they start a coffee-house near
by; to draw idle and listless young men from
the attractions of gambling hells, they open
lecture halls and free reading rooms; the ex-
hilaration of healthful exercise in the gymna-
sium counteracts the excitement of the low
dance hall. They say to the young men of
our cities, not simply, " Don't go there," but,
" Do come here." To all thinking observers,
such facts as these must bring more or less
conviction that it is by supplying positive

right activities for our children that we suppress the wrong ones.

More than this, a negative method trains a child inevitably into a critical, pessimistic character very depressing to us all. For instance: a mother came to me in utter discouragement, saying: "What shall I do with my five-year-old boy? He is simply the personification of the word *won't.*" After the lesson was over, I walked home with her. A beautiful child, with golden curls and great dancing black eyes, came running out to meet us and with all the impulsive joy of childhood, threw his arms around her. What were her first words ? "Don't do that, James, you will muss mamma's dress." I had already suspected where the trouble lay; now I knew that I was right. In a moment it was: "Don't twist so, my son." "Don't make that noise." In the four or five minutes we stood at her steps, she had said *don't* five times. Can you wonder that when she said, "Run in the house now, Mamma is coming in a minute." he replied: "No, I don't want to." Such training developes unduly the critical faculty and criticism leads to separation from our fellow-beings. Therefore, care must be taken, not only that the child himself be not over-criticised, but also that other people shall not be criticised in his presence; he is injured far more than they are helped. Unless some principle is involved, let the people about him pass for heroes and heroines.

Again, a year or two ago, I was visiting at a friend's house, when in the course of conversation, she said: "I do not know what is the difficulty in my sister's family. She tries to train her children aright, and yet they are almost unmanageable." The difficulty was revealed to me in a call made soon after. The mother sat with her two-year-old babe on her lap. She told me that the child could say only a few words; that he was not yet able to talk. Two of her children were playing in another part of the room. In a short time they became rather boisterous. The mother did not notice it, but the two-year-old turned around and in an impatient tone called out: "Boys ' top'." Here was the trouble. Babies, like parrots, learn to say first the words which they most frequently hear. Consequently this little one must have repeatedly heard the words, "Boys, stop!" which was merely the suppression of some annoying or wrong thing, and not a substitution of a right one in its place. It had not been: "Boys, run out in the yard and gather some flowers for the tea-table," or, "Boys, go up stairs and finish your sawing," or some like directing of their energy, but merely, " Boys, stop!" So they had undoubtedly "stopped" one prohibited thing and gone to another.

We find the same elements in literature. In my opinion such teachers as George Eliot are not healthful factors in the spiritual growth of young lives. Do not such writers emphasize the discordant side of life, rather than the harmonious one? In one of the numbers of the *British Review*, the author just spoken of has given to the world the true standard of measurement for a great writer. She says: " We do not value a writer in proportion to his freedom from faults, but in proportion to his positive excellences, to the variety of thought he contributes or suggests, *to the amount of gladdening and energizing emotion he excites.*" *This* is in accordance with Froebel's doctrines, but her literary work failed to rise to the height of her insight. If we take her own words as the test, what must be the judgment of the reader who, as he turn the last page of " Middlemarch," realizes that every worthy or lovable character in it has been so warped and marred by circumstances, that admiration has half turned into loving pity. "Daniel Deronda" and her other books leave us in the same depressed state. From this standpoint, must we not admit that the great English woman is not as helpful or as wholesome as many a writer who has far less brain power and artistic skill than she, but who leaves us with a strong feeling that right rules in God's universe? Emerson has said: "Even Schopenhauer preaching pessimism is odious."

If the power of optimism is so great in literature, it is even greater in life. The positive method of training builds up the cheering, optimistic character which is so much needed. Who are the men and women that are lifting the world upward and onward? Are they not those who *encourage more than they criticise?* who *do* more than they *undo?* The strongest, most beautiful characters are those who see the good that is in each person, who think the best that is possible of everyone, who as soon as they form a new acquaintance see his finest characteristics. The Kindergarten world gives innumerable illustrations of how this type of character may be developed.

A small child was brought to me who was the most complete embodiment of the result of

negative training with which I have ever come
in contact. It was, " No, I don't want to
play;" "No, I won't sit by that boy"; "No, I
don't like the blocks." It was one continual
" No." No one pleased him; nothing satisfied
him. Though not yet five years old, he was
already an isolated character, unhappy himself
and constantly making others uncomfortable.
I saw that the child needed more than anything else positive encouragement, to be led
into a spirit of participation with others. The
third day after his arrival another child
chanced to bring a small pewter soldier to the
Kindergarten. As is usual with each little
treasure brought from home, it was examined
and admired and at play-time it was allowed to
choose a game. This last privilege brought
to the new boy's face a look of contempt, which
sharply contrasted with the happy, sympathetic faces of the other children. Soon after we
had taken our places at the work-tables with
the toy-soldier standing erect in front of little
Paul, his proud owner, I heard a whizzing
sound and Paul's voice crying out: " Joseph
has knocked my soldier off the table and he
did it on purpose, too!" I turned to the scene
of disaster; the soldier lay on the other side of
the room, and Joseph, the iconoclastic inva-

der into our realm of peace, with defiance in his face, sat looking at me. The first impulse was to say: "Why did you do that? It was naughty; go and pick up the soldier." That, however, would have been another negation added to the number which had already been daily heaped upon him, so, instead, I said, "Oh well, Paul, never mind. Joseph does not know that we try to make each other happy in kindergarten."

"Come here, Joseph, I want you to be my messenger boy." The role of messenger boy, or helper to distribute the work, is always a much-coveted office; partly, from an inborn delight in children to assist in the work of older people; partly, from the distinction which arises in the imaginary wearing of the brass buttons and gilt band. As if expecting some hidden censure Joseph came a little reluctantly to where I was sitting. In a few minutes he was busy running back and forth giving to each child the envelope containing the work of the next half hour. As soon as the joy of service had melted him into a mood of comradeship, I whispered: "Run over now and get Paul's soldier." Instantly he ran across the room, picked up the toy and placing it on the table before its rightful owner, quietly slipped into his own place and began his work. His whole nature for the time being was changed into good-humored fellowship with all mankind.

Similar opportunities for like transformations may be found in the home life. A friend came to me and said: "What shall I do with my Willie? He dallies so about everything that he has to do. If I send him upstairs after my thimble or thread, it may be a half hour or even an hour before he returns. I have scolded him and scolded him, but it seems to do no good."

"By scolding," I replied, "you have emphasized the fault you wished to cure and have separated yourself from your boy. Now, try to emphasize the opposite virtue, promptness, by praising him for it when you have the opportunity."

"Oh, there's no use in talking of that," she answered, "he is never prompt."

"Then," said I, "if he is never so voluntarily, make an occasion. Ask him to go to the kitchen, or some other part of the house on an errand for you; tell him that you will count while he is gone. When he gets back, praise him for having returned more quickly than usual. At dinner tell his father as if it were a fine bit of news. This will make it a meritorious achievement in your son's eyes."

The next week she came to me with her face fairly radiant and said: "I have been counting and Willie has been trotting ever since last week." I laughed and told her that her mother-wit would soon have to hunt up some new device.

In Harriet Martineau's "Household Education" is a chapter on "Reverence." She shows how a child, lacking this virtue, should not be constantly criticised for his disrespect or irreverence, but instead needs to have his eyes opened to the wonders of creation, that the majesty and power of God displayed in His works may fill his heart with awe and hush it into the needed reverence. On the other hand, the child who is fearful and timid, over-reverent, really superstitious, ought not to be laughed at and ridiculed, but to have the power which is within himself developed, until courage and self-reliance restore the lacking balance to his character. This method of treatment bears at once practical results.

Many a mother says earnestly to herself: "What shall I do with my half-grown boy, his tone and manner are so lacking in respect? Or, the troublesome girl who almost defies

authority." Reproof but calls forth a pert reply, perhaps long argument which establishes
something of equality between parent and
child. The real question is not how to suppress this lack of respect for authority, but
how to develop the opposite virtue. One of
the favorite sayings of Dr. William T. Harris,
the well-known educator, is this: that every
man has two selves, the great self of humanity
and the institutional world, and the little self
of individuality. Such a child should learn
to compare his great self with his individual
self, then egotism and self-assertion will cease.
What has he done, compared with the achieve-
ments of mankind? What are his rights,
when the rights of the State at large are examined? All true patriotism, which demands
the glad laying down of life for country, arises
from the realization of this larger self.

With this principle in mind, let the mother
study the line of thought which most attracts
her child, that he may perceive that she has a
deeper, stronger grasp of the subject than he
can at present hope to have. As a rule, children worship skill of brain or hand. To illustrate: a mother completely cured her eight-
year-old daughter of a spirit of contradiction
by reading ahead of the child some books on

Natural History, and telling the contents to her in their daily walks. The girl soon learned to look up to the mother as a marvel of wisdom and authority on all Natural History subjects, and the feeling of respect in this realm was easily transferred to others. Over and over again have I seen similar changes brought about in a child's attitude towards older people, by like training.

Mothers, so cultivate the rational element in yourselves, that you can see that every fault in your child is simply the lack of some virtue. In the inner chamber of your own souls study your children; confess their faults to yourselves, not to your neighbors, and ask what is lacking that these defects exist. Like Nehemiah of old, build up the wall where it is the weakest; if your child is selfish, it is unselfishness he needs; if he is untruthful, it is accuracy which is lacking; perhaps he is tyrannical to the younger brother or sister; it is the element of nurture or tenderness which should be developed.

There is one caution which must be given in regard to the matter of approval. One should be sure the effort is a genuine one, else commendation will foster a species of hypocrisy which is worse than the fault sought to be eradicated.

Dante in his Divine Comedy places heathen philosophers and poets in Limbo, a place neither heaven nor hell, but he gives them the privilege of appreciating the *merits* of the lost souls as they pass along.   This is enough to make of Limbo, or any other spot, a heaven. You have it in your power to place this heaven within your child, and nothing on earth can entirely quench the happiness it will create.

CHAPTER II.

THE INSTINCT OF INVESTIGATION, OR THE TRAIN-
ING OF THE SENSES.

There is perhaps no instinct of the child more important and less guarded than the exercise of his senses. The inner being awakes by means of the impressions conveyed to the young brain through those avenues. The baby begins this life-work as soon as his eyes can fix themselves on any point in space, as soon as his tiny hand can grasp any object of the material world. Although, in reality, the three-fold nature of the child cannot be separated, for the sake of closer study we may consider the subject from three standpoints: first, the physical value; second, the intellectual value; third, the moral value of the right training of the senses.

The one thing which prevents most of us from being that which we might have been, is the dull, stupid way in which we have used our senses. Thousands of us having eyes to see, see not; having ears to hear, hear not; in the literal, as well as the spiritual, sense

of the words.   Question any two persons who
have listened to the same sermon or lecture,
and you will discover how much one has heard
which has escaped the other.   Talk with any
intelligent acquaintance about a picture gallery
or a foreign city, which you both have visited, and you will be covered with chagrin
by the realization of how much you did not
see.

"The artist," says George Eliot, "becomes
the true teacher by giving us his higher sensi-
bilities as a medium, a delicate acoustic or
optical instrument, bringing home to our
coarser senses that which would otherwise be
unperceived by us."   The joy which comes
from a sunset cloud, the happiness which the
song of a bird may produce, the poetry and
glory of all creation lie unseen about us because these windows of the soul have not been
opened.

Half the wealth of the world is lost to
most of us from lack of power to perceive.
The difference between so-called clever children
and intelligent ones is largely a difference in
their sense-perception.   For the purpose of
training aright these much-neglected instruments, the Kindergarten has games in which
first one sense and then another is exercised

and strengthened. For example, the child is allowed to shut his eyes and by touch to tell the name of an object, or from his hearing to tell the object struck and what struck it, or by taste or smell to describe and name the thing placed before him. But the teacher or mother who realizes the *higher* need does not let the child rest in the mere *sense-impression.* He is given two objects that he may contrast them, or he hears two differing sounds, smells two odors, tastes two flavors, and is led to contrast the one with the other, that the higher faculty of comparison may also be developed by the play. Thus the little ears learn to hear soft notes that our duller ones can not catch; thus the young eyes learn to recognize finer shades of color than our less trained ones can perceive.

The habit of contrasting or comparing in material things leads to a fineness of distinction in higher matters. John Ruskin and like thinkers claim that a perception of and love for the beautiful in nature leads directly into a discernment of the beautiful in the moral world.

The *intellectual* value of a clear and definite training of the senses is usually perceived by any thinking mind. The child who has early

learned to notice the difference between sweet
and sour, between smooth and rough, between
straight and crooked in material things, is the
sooner able to transfer the meaning to intellectual qualities. He more readily understands the
meaning of " sweet disposition," "sour temper,"
" smooth manner," " rough speech," " straight
conduct," " crooked dealings," and the like.
Children begin to make this higher use of their
vocabulary as soon as they thoroughly comprehend the physical meaning of the word. Occasionally they put the object into the new sentence, often making laughable mistakes, and
reminding the listener of the days of the childhood of the race, when a brave chieftain was
called a lion man, the shrewd leader was named
the fox.   One morning we had hyacinth bulbs;
we examined them and compared them with
some blossoming hyacinths which stood upon
the window-sill.   A day or two after, an onion
was brought in by a delighted child, as another
fat round flower-baby for us to plant.   I had
some difficulty in making them see the difference, and finally cut the onion open, and, blind-
ing their eyes, let them smell first the flower
and then the onion bulb. An hour or two later
one of the little girls spoke in an irritated, petulant tone to her neighbor who had accident-

ally knocked over her blocks. "Look out," said
a little one the other side of her, "or you'll
have *an onion voice* soon!" The sense of this
child had not been sufficiently trained to enable
her to *abstract* or detach the property "disagreeable" from the object, so the entire onion
had to be dragged into her warning. The
sooner the child is freed from the necessity of
using objects to express his thought, the sooner
he becomes able to communicate his inner
thought to the outer world. When he learns
the finer distinctions of the physical properties
of matter, his vocabulary becomes enriched ten-
fold, and he obtains that much-needed, much-
coveted gift, "the power of utterance," for the
lack of which most of us go like dumb creatures about the world, so far as the giving forth
of our higher selves is concerned.

The *moral* value of the complete control of
the senses has not been so universally recognized. Bain and other authorities on mental
science divide the senses into two groups;
first, the lower: taste, smell, and touch, as related to organic life, *i. e.* hunger, thirst, reple-
tion, suffocation, warmth, and other sensations
whose office relates to the upbuilding of the
body; and second, the higher: touch proper,
hearing and sight, or those which relate to

the outside world.   The former are called the *lower* senses from the fact that they aid less directly the mental growth, by producing less vivid pictures in the mind.   For instance, the remembrance called forth by the words "sweet apple," or "odor of violets," is not so distinct as that given by the words, "large apple," "blue violets."   To a limited extent the world at large has acknowledged this distinction, intellectually, between the lower and the higher senses, has directed the training of the eye and the ear, and is now struggling to place in the school curriculum a systematized teaching of the sense of touch.   But the overwhelming *moral* need of mankind lies in the world of the lower senses.   The non-training of these is exceedingly dangerous because they have direct effect upon the will.   Any child turns more quickly from a bad *odor* than from a bad *picture*, comes with more alacrity to get a *sweetmeat* than to hear some *pleasing sound*.   Is it not the same with most adults?   Are not the invitations to dinner more frequently accepted than those to hear fine music?   Are not our sympathies aroused more readily by a tale of physical suffering than by one of demoralizing surroundings?   Notwithstanding these facts, the two lower senses of taste and smell have been left almost entirely to the haphazard education of circumstances. Sad indeed have been the results.

As we look abroad over the world, what do we perceive to be the chief cause of the wrecks and ruins, of the wretchedness and misery which lie about us? Why have we on every hand such dwarfed and stunted characters? For what reason do crimes, too polluting to be mentioned save where remedy is sought, poison our moral atmosphere until our great cities become fatal to half the young men and women who come to them? Why do our clergy and other reformers have to labor so hard to attract the hearts of men to what is in itself glorious and beautiful?·

Is it not, in a majority of cases, *because mankind has not learned to subordinate the gratification of physical appetite to rational ends?* It is to be seen in every phase of society; from the rich and favored dame, so enervated by soft chairs and tempered lights and luxurious surroundings that she is blind to the sight of misery and deaf to the cry of despair, down through the grades where we find the luxuries of the table the only luxuries indulged in, and "plain living and high thinking" the exception, still farther down from these respectable

phases of self-indulgence to t   poor drunkard
who sacrifices all comforts of the home, all
peace of the family life, for the gratification of
his insatiable thirst, down to the pitiable wretch
who sells her soul that her body may live.

Do not their lives, all of them, contradict
that significant question of the Son of God:
" Is not the body more than the raiment?" " Is
not the life more than the meat?"

Let us turn from these distressing pictures
to seek such remedy as the scientific investigation of the senses may offer.

The sense of taste has two offices, relish and
power to discriminate; the first, for the producing of certain pleasant sensations in the
mouth or stomach, and the second, for the judg-
ing between wholesomeness and unwholesomeness of food, the latter being *taste proper*.

The *former* is the gratification of the sense
for the sake of the sensation, and leads through
over-indulgence directly into gluttony, which,
in its turn, leads into sensuality.   In history
not until a nation begins to send far and wide
for delicacies and condiments for its markets
and tables does it become voluptuous and sensual. When we speak of " the degenerate days
of Rome " do not pictures of their over-loaded
tables rise before the mind's eye?

We need not have turned to other times for illustrations of this truth. Who are the " high livers" of to-day? Are they not too often sensualists as well?

The *latter* use of this organ of sensation leads to discrimination, which discrimination produces wholesome restraint upon undue eating; this restraint engenders self-control, making the *moral will-power over the bodily appetite*— man's greatest safeguard in the hour of temptation. In the physical world, we know that rank vegetation needs to be pruned and checked if it is to give to man its best fruits; thus nature teaches us *her* lesson.

In the intellectual world, the prophets and seers have always seen the close connection between the right feeding of the body and the control of the sensual appetites. Long ago Plato in " The Republic" would have all books banished which contained descriptions of the mere pleasures of food, drink, and love, classing the three under one head. What an enormous amount of so-called literature would have to be swept out of the libraries of to-day, were that mandate sent forth! Dante, with that marvelous vision of his which seemed to see through all disguises and all forms of sin back to the causes of the same, places gluttony and sensuality in the same circle of the Inferno. At least two great branches of the Christian church, the Roman Catholic and the Protestant Episcopal, have realized the moral value of placing the appetites under the control of the will, in their establishment and maintenance of the season of Lent. Let him who would scoff at the observance of this season of restraint, try for six weeks to go without his favorite article of food, and he will realize for himself the amount of will-power it requires. To me, the story of Daniel derives its significance, not so much from the fearless courage with which that "Great Heart" dared death in the lion's den, as from the fact that as a child he had moral control enough to turn from the king's sumptuous table and eat simple pulse and drink pure water. Such self-control *must* produce the courage and the manhood which will die for a principle. So, in telling this story, ever loved by childhood, we always emphasize the earlier struggle and victory rather than the later.

The perfect character is the character with the perfectly controlled will; therefore, the heroes of the Kindergarten stories are mightier than they who have taken a city, for they have conquered themselves. The greatest battles of the world are the battles which are fought within the human breast ; and, alas, the greatest defeats are here also !

A writer in a recent article in *The Christian Union* showed that a child's inheritance of certain likes and dislikes in the matter of food does not in the least forbid the training of his taste towards that which is healthful and upbuilding, it merely adds an element to be considered in the training.

Another gifted writer of our own nation, Horace Bushnell, in his book called " Christian Nurture " utters these impressive words: " The child is taken when his training begins, in a state of naturalness as respects all the bodily tastes and tempers, and the endeavor should be to keep him in that key, to let no stimulation of excess or delicacy disturb the simplicity of nature, and no sensual pleasure in the name of food become a want or expectation of his appetite. Any artificial appetite begun is the beginning of distemper, disease and a general disturbance of natural proportion. Intemperance ! The woes of intemperate drink ! how dismal the story, when it is told ; how dreadful the picture when we look upon it. From what do the father and mother recoil with a greater and more total horror of feeling, than the pos-

sibility that their child is to be a drunkard?
Little do they remember that he can be, even
before he has so much as tasted the cup ; and
that they themselves can make him so, virtual-
ly without meaning it, even before he has gotten his language.   Nine-tenths of the intemperate drinking begins, not in grief and desti-
tution, as we often hear, but in vicious *feeding.*
Here the scale and order of simplicity is first
broken, and then what shall a distempered or
distemperate life run to, more certainly than
what is intemperate? False feeding engenders
false appetite, and when the soul is burning all
through in the fires of false appetite, what is
that but a universal uneasiness? And what
will this uneasiness more actually do than par-
take itself to the pleasure and excitement of
drink?"   Much more that is suggestive and
helpful to the mother is given in his chapter
entitled "Physical Nurture to be a means of
Grace."

Froebel, from whose eagle eye nothing which
related to the child seemed to escape, saw this
danger, and in his "Education of Man" says:
"In the early years the child's food is a matter
of very great importance; not only may the
child by this means be made indolent or active,
sluggish or mobile, dull or bright, inert or

vigorous, but, indeed, *for his entire life.* Impressions, inclinations, appetites, which the child may have derived from his food, the turn it may have given to his senses and even to his life as a whole, can only with difficulty be set aside, even when the age of self-dependence has been reached ; they are one with his whole physical life, and therefore intimately connected with his spiritual life. And again, parents and nurses should ever remember, as underlying every precept in this direction, the following general principle: that simplicity and frugality in food and in other physical needs during the years of childhood enhance man's power of attaining happiness and vigor—true creativeness in every respect. Who has not noticed in children, overstimulated by spices and excesses of food, appetites of a very low order, from which they can never again be freed— appetites which, even when they seem to have been suppressed, only slumber, and in times of opportunity return with greater power, threatening to · rob man of all his dignity and to force him away from his duty."

Then comes with an almost audible sigh these words : "It is by far easier than we think to promote and establish the welfare of mankind. All the means are simple and at hand,

yet we see them not.   You see them perhaps,
but do not notice them.   In their simplicity,
availability, and nearness, they seem too insignificant, and we despise them.   We seek help
from afar, although help is only in and through
ourselves.   Hence, *at a later period half or all
our accumulated wealth can not procure for our
children what greater insight and keener vision
discern as their greatest good.*   This they must
miss, or enjoy but partially or scantily.   It
might have been theirs in full measure, had
we expended very much less for their physical
comfort."   Then he exclaims in ringing tones,
as the enormous significance of the subject
grows upon him: "Would that to each young
newly married couple there could be shown in
all its vividness, only one of the sad experiences and observations in its small and seemingly
insignificant beginnings, and in its incalculable
consequences that tend utterly to destroy all
the good of after education."

Next he points out the way to avoid the sad
consequences which he so laments. "And here
it is easy to avoid the wrong and to find the
right.   Always let the food be simply for
nourishment—never more, never less.   Never
should the food be taken for its own sake, but
for the sake of promoting bodily and mental

activity. Still less should the peculiarities of food, its taste or delicacy, ever become an object in themselves, but only a means to make it good, pure, wholesome nourishment; else in both cases the food destroys health. Let the food of the little child be as simple as the circumstances in which the child lives can afford, and let it be given in proportion to his bodily and mental activity."

There is no one among us who cannot recall pictures of young mothers putting a spoonful of sweet to the baby's mouth, and persuading that unwilling little one to take the unaccustomed food, saying with coaxing tone such words of encouragement as, " So good, so good," in this way teaching the child to dwell upon and value the relish side of his food.

Not long ago I had occasion to take a long ride on a street car. My attention was attracted to a placid mother with her year-old child in her arms. The little one was in quiet wonder looking out on the great, new world about him, with its myriads of moving objects. Here was a picture of serene contentment in both mother and child. Soon the mother slipped her hand into her pocket and drew forth a small paper bag, out of which she took a piece of candy and put it into her

mouth ; then, fearing, I suppose, that this
might be selfish, she took out another piece
and put it into the infant's mouth. The
child resented the intrusion upon its medita-
tions by ejecting the proffered sweet. The
mother was not to be defeated in her gener-
osity. She put it back into the child's mouth
and held it there until the little one began
to suck it of his own account. This operation was repeated a number of times, about
every third piece of candy being given to the
child. Once or twice the small recipient
turned its head away, but was coaxed back
by the cooing voice of the mother saying,
"Take it, darling; see, mamma likes candy,"
illustrating the remark by eating a piece and
giving every sign of enjoyment during the
operation. The child was soon won over, and
began to reach out his hands for more. After the unwholesome relish had been sufficiently accumulated in the delicate little stomach
to make the child physically uncomfortable,
he began to show a restlessness, a desire to
move about unnecessarily. The mother grew
impatient, which only increased the child's uneasiness; finally she shook him, saying, " I don't
see what in the world is the matter with you. You
are a bad troublesome little thing!" At this,

the unjustly accused little victim set up a lusty
yell, and the mother in a few minutes left the
c   great confusion and with a very red face,
wondering, no doubt, from which of his father's relatives the child inherited such a disagreeable disposition.

"But," exclaimed one mother to me, "do
you mean to say that you would not give any
confectionery to a child? *I* think candy is the
prerogative of all children. Why, I think it
is a crime to take it away from them!" "I
think," was my reply, "that a healthy body
and a strong moral will-power are the pre-
rogatives of each child, and it is a crime to
take *them* away from him." "But," she added,
in an annoyed tone, "I do love candy so myself, and I can't eat it before my child and
not give her a part of it!"

I do not mean that all sweets must be
banished from the nursery or the table,—the
child would thus be deprived of a lesson in
voluntary self-control ; but they should be
given as relishes only, after a wholesome meal,
letting the child understand that it adds little
or nothing to his up-building, and must, therefore, be taken sparingly.

In "The Tasting Song," in that wonderful
book of his for mothers, Froebel suggests that
4

the child's thoughts may be playfully led to the discrimination of different kinds of food and the value of the same. He says, " Who does not know and rejoice that you, dear mother, can carry on everything as a game with your child, and can dress up for him the most important things of life in charming play?"

It is not supposed that any mother will feel herself compelled to use the rather crude rhyme given in the "Mother Book," still it contains the needed hint of *playfully guiding the child's attention to the after effects of different kinds of food.* Froebel has said: "This is the way in which you, mother, try to foster, develop and improve each sense, playfully and gaily, but especially the sense of taste. What is more important for your child than the improvement of the senses, especially the improvement of the sense of taste, in its transferred moral meaning, as well." Farther on in the same earnest talk with the mother (see page 136 "Mother Songs ") he tells her that by such exercising of her child's senses does she teach him gradually to judge of the *inner essence* of things by their *appearance*; that it is not necessary for any one to actually indulge in wrong-doing, claiming that moral as well as physical things show their real nature to the observing eye. Thus if the child is trained to know the wholesomeness or unwholesomeness of food by its results or after effects, he will the more readily judge of the nature of a pleasure, of a companion, of a book, of a line of conduct, by its after effects; and it is not, therefore, necessary that he "sow his wild oats," or "see the world," in the pitiable sense in which that term is used, in order that he may know life. His rational judgment can teach him what, oftentimes, sad, bitter, deforming experiences tell him, alas! too late to avoid. Most of you are familiar with the old Greek story of Perseus,—how, when commanded by the king to bring the head of the slain Medusa to the court, the wise young Perseus took with him a bright and shining shield in which he could see *reflected* the image of the terrible Gorgon, learn what manner of creature she was, know her exact whereabouts, and study how best to destroy her, without himself coming in personal contact with her, for well he knew fatal to him would be that contact. The legend tells us that he thereby returned triumphant to court, having destroyed the destroyer. This to me is one of the most significant of all the old Greek myths.

In the motto of this "Tasting Song" Froebel says to the mother:

> " Ever through the senses Nature woos the child,
>   Thou canst help him comprehend her lessons mild."

In other words, *Nature, God's instrument, is striving to educate your child spiritually.* You are another of His instruments, dull or sharp, according to the care you are giving to this physical training.

> " By the senses is the inner door unsealed,
>   Where the spirit glows in light revealed."

Froebel's convictions on this subject are definite. That the soul, the Divine element in each child, is, as it were, sealed up when he first comes into the world, and is gradually awakened and strengthened by the impressions which come to him through the senses from the outside world; that the physical and spiritual growth of the child go forward, not only simultaneously, but the one by means of the other. He especially charges the mother to teach her child *to observe and avoid things which are unripe.* " Make your child notice not only the fixed steps of development from the unripe to the ripe, but above all have him realize that to use *what is unripe is contrary to Nature in all relations and conditions of life,* and often works, in its turn, injuriously on life, on physical but no less on intellectual and social life;" and as a closing word he exclaims, "If you do this, you will be really, as a mother, one of the greatest benefactors of the human race."

That the opinions and consequently the actions of children are easily influenced through play, becomes evident to any one who has ever played much with them. One morning, while giving a lesson with the building blocks, we made an oblong form, which I asked one of the children to name. "It is a table—a breakfast table." "Let us play they are all breakfast tables," said I; "I will come around and visit each one and see what the little children have to eat. What is on your table, Helen?" "Oh!" exclaimed she, with eager delight, "my children have ice-cream and cake and soda-water and—" "Oh, dear! oh, dear!" cried I, holding up my hands, "poor little things! just think of their having such a thoughtless mamma, who didn't know how to give them good, wholesome food for their breakfast! How can they ever grow big and strong on such stuff as that? What is on your table Frank?" "My children have bread and butter, oatmeal and cream, and baked potatoes," said the discreet young father.

"Ah!" said I, in a tone of intense satisfaction, "now here is a sensible mamma, who knows how to take care of her children!" "Oh," broke in little Helen, "my children's mamma came into the room and when she saw what they were eating she *jerked* the ice-cream off the table." The significant gesture which accompanied the emphatic tone told of the sudden revolution which had taken place in the child's mind as to the right kinds of food for carefully reared children.

In a thousand such ways can children be influenced to form judgments concerning lines of conduct which will help them to decide aright when the real deed is to be enacted. I know of the Kindergarten-trained five-year-old son of a millionaire, who refused spiced pickles, when they were passed to him at the table. "Why, my son," said his father, "do you not wish some pickles? They are very nice." "No," replied the boy, "I don't see any use in eating spiced pickles. It doesn't help to make me any stronger; my teacher says it doesn't." If this kind of training can be carried out, such a childhood will grow into a young manhood which, when tempted, can easily say, "No. I see no use in that. It will help to make me neither a stronger nor a better man."

Almost any Kindergartner will tell you that children are easily trained to prefer wholesome to unwholesome food, even when all the home influences are against the training. I had charge one year of a class of children who were indulged in their home life in almost every respect. On one occasion an injudicious mother sent to the Kindergarten a very large birthday cake, richly ornamented with candied fruits and other sweets. In cutting the cake, I quite incidentally said: "We do not wish to upset any of our stomachs with these sweets, so we will lay them aside," suiting the action to the word. After each child had eaten a good sized slice of the cake (a privilege always allowed on a birthday), there was at least one-third of it left. Not a child out of the twenty asked for a second piece, nor for a bit of the confectionery. This was not because they were in any way suppressed, or afraid to make their wishes known, for they felt almost absolutely free and were accustomed to ask for anything desired; it was simply that, through previous plays, talks and stories, they had learned that I did not approve of such things for children, so when with me *they* did not either. Thus, easily and imperceptibly are little children moulded. The mother who holds herself responsible for what her child shall wear, and yet does not feel that she is answerable for what he shall eat, shows that she regards his outer appearance more than his health of body or moral strength.

The danger of wrong training lies not alone in the indulgence of the sense of taste. Testimony is not wanting of the evil effects of the cultivation of the relish side of the other senses also. After giving a lesson on the training of the senses to a class in Chicago, a stranger to me introduced herself as having formerly been a missionary to the Sandwich Islands. "This lesson has explained," said she, "a custom among the Sandwich Islanders, which I never before understood. When the natives begin their religious rites and ceremonies, which, you know, are very licentious, the women are in the habit of decking themselves with wreaths of orange blossoms and other flowers, which have a strongly agreeable scent, until the air is heavy with the odor."

"Do you not know who are usually the over-perfumed women of our land?" asked I. "And yet I know scores of mothers who unconsciously train their children to revel in an excessive indulgence in perfumery."

Mr. William Tomlins, a man who has almost regenerated the musical world for children, once said, in a talk on musical education: "If music ends only in fitting us to enjoy it ourselves, it becomes selfishly enervating, *and this reacts on the musical tone.*" Therefore, he has long made a habit of teaching the hundreds of children who come under his instruction, to sing sweetly and to enunciate clearly, that they may be worthy of singing at this or that concert for the benefit of some grand charity. The dissipation which is seen in the lives of so many of this most ennobling profession is thus easily explained. Their music has been carried forward with too little thought of the pleasure it could give to others.

Nor does this far-reaching thought stop with the right and wrong training of the senses. The mother who praises her child's curls or rosy cheeks rather than the child's actions or inner motives, is developing the relish side of character—placing beauty of appearance over and above beauty of conduct. The father who takes his boy to the circus, and, passing by the menagerie and acrobat's skill, teaches the boy to enjoy the clown and like parts of the exhibition, is leading to the development of the relish side of amusement, and is training the child to regard excitement and recreation as necessarily one and the same thing.

Fashionable parties for children, those abom-
inations upon the face of the earth, are but sea-
soned condiments of that most wholesome food
for the young soul, social contact with its
peers. That so simple, so sweet, so holy,
and so necessary a thing as the commingling of
little children in play and work with those of
their own age and ability, should be twisted
and turned into an artificial fashionable party,
seems, to the real lover of childhood, incredi-
ble, save for the sad fact that it is.

Even our Sunday Schools, with their prizes
and exhibitions and sensational programs, are
not exempt from the crime. I have seen the holy
Easter festival so celebrated by Sunday Schools
that, so far as its effects upon the younger
children were concerned, they might each one
as well have been given a glass of intoxicating
liquor, so upset was their digestion, so excited
their brains, so demoralized their unused emotions.

Need I speak of the relish side of the dress
of children? John Ruskin, the great apostle
of the beautiful, claims that no ornament is
beautiful which has not a use.

The relish, perhaps, whose demoralizing influence is beginning to be suspected, is that of
highly-seasoned literature, if we may call such

writing by the name of that which stands for all that is best of the thoughts and experiences of the human race. Mothers and teachers can not too earnestly sift the reading matter of the children of whom they have charge. There are, aside from the text books needed in their school work, some few great books which have stood the test of time and critics. Teach your children to understand and to love these. Above all, as a means of culture, as well as a means of inspiration and a guide to conduct, would I recommend that book of books, the Bible, to be the constant companion of mother and child.

Some may fall into the minor danger of teaching the child too great discrimination, until he becomes an epicure. The child who pushes away his oatmeal because it has milk instead of cream over it, is in a fair way to grow into the man who will push away the mass of humanity because they are unwashed. God pity him if he does!

I once knew of a call which came from a large and needy district to a young woman who seemingly longed, with all her heart, to be of use in the world. "But," said she to me, "I cannot possibly go; the salary is only seven hundred dollars, and that would not pay even for the necessaries of life with me." So she continues to live a barren, unsatisfied life.

I knew another fine-brained, beautiful woman, whose insight was far beyond her times, to whom there came a grand opportunity to advance a great cause. "I cannot," she said despairingly, "do without my china and cut-glass, the *disease of luxury* has fast hold upon me." "S   train your child," says Emerson, "that at the age of thirty or forty, he shall not have to say, 'This great thing could I do but for the lack of tools.'" So train him, I would add, that he shall not have to say, "All my time and strength is spent in obtaining super-fluities, which have become necessities to me." Goethe teaches us this great lesson in his drama of Faust. He who studies attentively this marvelous poem can be saved the sad fate of becoming a Faust in order that he may solve "the Faust problem." With master strokes is drawn the picture, which shows that no gratification of human appetite, passion or ambition, brings in itself satisfaction and rest, but he alone who lives for others as well as for himself can truly say unto his life, "Ah, still delay—thou art so fair."

CHAPTER III.

THE MIND.

THE INSTINCT OF POWER, OR THE TRAINING OF THE EMOTIONS.

Old Homer, back in the past ages, shows us a charming picture of Nausicaa and her maidens, after a hard day's washing, resting themselves with a game of ball. Thus we see this most free and graceful plaything connected with that free and beautifully developed nation which has been the admiration of the world ever since. Plato has said, "The plays of children have the mightiest influence on the maintenance or non-maintenance of laws;" and again, "During earliest childhood, the soul of the nursling should be made cheerful and kind, by keeping away from him sorrow and fear and pain, by soothing him with sound of the pipe and of rhythmical movement." He still further advised that the children should be brought to the temples, and allowed to play under the supervision of nurses, presumably trained for that purpose. Here we see plainly foreshadowed the Kindergarten, whose foundation is "education by play"; as the study of the Kindergar-

ten system leads to the earnest, thoughtful
consideration of the office of play, and the
exact value which the plaything or toy has in
the development of the child ; when this is
once understood, the choice of what toys to give
to children is easily made.

In the world of nature, we find the blossom
comes before the fruit; in history, art arose
long before science was possible; in the human
race, the emotions are developed sooner than
the reason. With the individual child it is the
same; the childish heart opens spontaneously
in play, the barriers are down, and the loving
mother or the wise teacher can find entrance
into the inner court as in no other way. The
child's *sympathies* can be attracted towards an
object, person, or line of conduct, much earlier
than his reason can grasp any one of them.
His emotional nature can and does receive impressions long before his intellectual nature is
ready for them; in other words, he can *love* before he can *understand*.

One of the mistakes of our age is, that we
begin by educating our children's *intellects*
rather than their *emotions*. We leave these all-
powerful factors, which give to life its coloring
of light or darkness, to the oftentimes insuffi-
cient training of the ordinary family life—in-

sufficient, owing to its thousand interruptions and preoccupations. The results are, that many children grow up cold, hard, matter-of-fact, with little of poetry, sympathy, or ideality to enrich their lives,—mere Gradgrinds in God's world of beauty. We starve the healthful emotions of children in order that we may overfeed their intellects. Is not this doing them a great wrong? When the sneering tone is heard, and the question "Will it pay?" is the all-important one, do we not see the result of such training? Possibly the unwise training of the emotional nature may give it undue preponderance, producing morbid sentimentalists, who think that the New Testament would be greatly improved if the account of Christ driving the money-changers from the temple, or His denunciation of the Pharisees, could be omitted. Such people feed every able-bodied tramp brought by chance to their doors, and yet make no effort to lighten the burden of the poor sewing-women of our great cities, who are working at almost starvation prices. This is a minor danger, however. The education of the heart must advance along with that of the head, if well-balanced character is to be developed.

Pedagogy tells us that "*the science of educa-*

tion is the science of interesting;" and yet, but few pedagogues have realized the importance of *educating the interest of the child.*   In other words, little or no value has been attached to the likes and dislikes of children; but in reality they are very important.

A child can be given any quantity of information, he can be made to get his lessons, he can even be crowded through a series of examinations, but that is not *educating* him.   Unless his interest in the subject has been awakened, the process has been a failure.   *Once get him thoroughly interested and he can educate himself, along that line, at least.*

Hence the value of toys; they are not only promoters of play, but they appeal to the sympathies and give exercise to the emotions; in this way a hold is gotten upon the child, by interesting him before more intellectual training can make much impression. The two great obstacles to the exercise of the right emotions are *fear* and *pity;* these do not come into the toy-world, hence we can see how toys, according to their own tendencies, help in the healthful education of the child's emotions, through his emotions the education of his thoughts, through his thoughts the education of his will, and hence his character.

One can readily see how this is so. By means of their dolls, wagons, drums, or other toys, children's thoughts are turned in certain directions. They play that they are mothers and fathers, or shop-keepers, or soldiers, as the case may be. Through their dramatic play, they become interested more and more in those phases of life which they have imitated, and that which they watch and imitate they become like.

The toy-shops of any great city are, to him who can read the signs of the times, prophecies of the future of that city. They not only predict the future career of a people, but they tell us of national tendencies. Seguin, in his report on the Educational exhibit at Vienna a few years ago, said: "The nations which had the most toys had, too, more individuality, ideality, and heroism." And again: "The nations which have been made famous by their artists, artisans, and idealists, supplied their infants with toys." It needs but a moment's thought to recognize the truth of this statement. Children who have toys exercise their *own* imagination, put into action their *own* ideals— Ah me, how much that means! What ideals have been strangled in the breasts of most of us because others did not think as we did! With the toy, an outline only is drawn ; the child must

5

fill in the details. On the other hand, in story books the details are given. Both kinds of training are needed; individual development, and participation in the development of others— of the world, of the past, of the *All.* With this thought of the influence of toys upon the life of nations, a visit to any large toy-shop becomes an interesting and curious study. The following is the testimony, unconsciously given, by the shelves and counters in one of the large importing establishments which gather together and send out the playthings of the world. The *French* toys include nearly all the pewter soldiers, all guns and swords; surely, such would be the toys of the nation which produced a Napoleon. All Punch and Judy shows are of French manufacture; almost all miniature theatres; all doll tea-sets which have wine glasses and finger bowls attached. The French *dolls* mirror the fashionable world, with all its finery and unneeded luxury, and hand it down to the little child. No wonder Frances Willard made a protest against dolls, if she had in mind the *French* doll.

"You see," said the guileless saleswoman, as she handed me first one and then another of these dolls, thinking doubtless that she had a slow purchaser whom she had to assist in making a selection, "you can dress one of these dolls as a lady, or as a little girl, just as you like." And, sure enough, the very baby dolls had upon their faces the smile of the society flirt, or the deep passionate look of the woman who had seen the world. I beheld the French Salons of the eighteenth century still lingering in the nineteenth century dolls. All their toys are dainty, artistic, exquisitely put together, but lack strength and power of endurance, are low or shallow in aim, and are oftentimes inappropriate in the extreme. For instance, I was shown a Noah's Ark with a rose-window of stained glass in one end of it. Do we not see the same thing in French literature? Racine's Orestes, bowing and complimenting his Iphigenia, is the same French adornment of the strong, simple, Greek story that the pretty window was of the Hebrew Ark.

The *German* toys take another tone. They are heavier, stronger, and not so artistic, and largely represent the home and the more primitive forms of trade-life. From Germany we get all our ready-made doll-houses, with their clean tile floors and clumsy porcelain stoves, their parlors with round iron center-tables, and stiff, ugly chairs with the inevitable lace tidies. Here and there in these miniature houses we

see a tiny pot of artificial flowers. All such
playthings tend to draw the child's thoughts
to the home-life. Next come the countless
number of toy butcher shops, bakers, black-
smiths, and other representations of the small,
thrifty, healthful trade-life which one sees all
over Germany. Nor is the child's love attracted toward the home and the shops alone.
Almost all of the better class of toy horses and
carts are of German manufacture. The " woolly
sheep," so dear to childish heart, is of the same
origin. Thus a love for simple, wholesome
out-of-door activities is instilled.

And then the German dolls! One would
know from the dolls alone that Germany was
the land of Froebel and the birthplace of the
Kindergarten, that it was the country where
even the beer-gardens are softened and refined
by the family presence. All the regulation
ornaments for Christmas trees come from this
nation, bringing with them memories of Luther;
of his breaking away from the celibacy en-
joined by the church; of his entering into the
joyous family life, and trying to bring with him
into the home life all that was sacred in the
church—Christmas festivals along with the
rest. Very few firearms come from this nation,
but among them I saw some strong cast-iron

cannons from Berlin; they looked as if Bismarck himself might have ordered their manufacture.

The *Swiss* toys are largely the bluntly carved wooden cattle, sheep and goats, with equally blunt shepherds and shepherdesses, reminding one forcibly of the dull faces of those much-enduring beasts of burden called Swiss peasants. I once saw a Swiss girl who had sold to an American woman, for a few francs, three handkerchiefs, the embroidering of which had occupied the evenings of her entire winter; there was no look of discontent or disgust as the American tossed them into her trunk with a lot of other trinkets, utterly oblivious of the amount of human life which had been patiently worked into them. What kind of toys could come from a people among whom such scenes are accepted as a matter of course?

The *English* rag doll is peculiarly national in its placidity of countenance. The British people stand pre-eminent in the matter of story books for children, but, so far as I have been able to observe, are somewhat lacking in originality as to toys; possibly this is due to the out-of-door life encouraged among them.

When I asked to see the *American* toys, my guide turned, and with a sweep of her hand said: "These *trunks* are American. All doll-

trunks are manufactured in this country."
Surely our Emerson was right when he said
that "the tape-worm of travel was in every
American." Here we see the beginning of the
restless, migratory spirit of our people; even
these children's toys suggest, "How nice it
would be to pack up and go somewhere!" All
tool-chests are of domestic origin. Seemingly,
all the inventions of the Yankee mind are reproduced in miniature form to stimulate the
young genius of our country.

The *Japanese* and *Chinese* toys are a curious
study, telling of national traits as clearly as do
their laws or their religion. They are endur-
able, made to last unchanged a long time ; no
flimsy tinsel is used which can be admired for
the hour, then cast aside. If "the hand of
Confucius reaches down through twenty-four
centuries of time still governing his people,"
so, too, can the carved ivory or inlaid wooden
toy be used without injury or change by
at least one or two successive generations of
children.

Let us turn to the study of the development
of the race as a whole, that we may the better
grasp this thought. The toy not only directs
the emotional activity of the child, but also
forms a bridge between the great realities of

life and his small capacities. To man was given the dominion over the earth, but it was a potential dominion. He had to conquer the beasts of the field; to develop the resources of the earth; by his *own effort*, to subordinate all things else unto himself. We see the faint foreshadowing, or presentiment, of this in the myths and legends of the race. The famous wooden horse of Troy, accounts of which have come down to us in a dozen different channels of literature and history, seems to have been the forerunner of the nineteenth century bomb, which defies walls and leaps into the enemy's camp, scattering death and destruction in every direction. At least, the two have the same effect; they speedily put an end to physical resistance, and bring about consultation and settlement by arbitration. The labors of Hercules tell the same story in another form—man's power to make nature perform the labors appointed to him; the winged sandals of Hermes, Perseus' cloak of invisibility, the armor of Achilles, and a hundred other charming myths, all tell us of man's sense of his sovereignty over nature. The old Oriental stories of the enchanted carpet tell us that the sultan and his court had but to step upon it, ere it rose majestically and sailed unimpeded through the air,

and landed its precious freight at the desired
destination.   Is not this the dim feeling in the
breasts of the childish race that *man* ought to
have power to transcend space, and by his intelligence contrive to convey himself from place
to place?   Are not our luxurious palace cars
almost fulfilling these early dreams?   What
are the fairy tales of the Teutonic people, which
Grimm has so laboriously collected for us?
They have lived through centuries of time,
because they have told of genii and giant, gov-
erned by the will of puny man and made to do
his bidding.   Eagerly the race has read them,
pleased to see symbolically pictured forth man's
power over elements stronger than himself. In
fact, the study of the race development is
much like the study of those huge, almost-
obliterated outlines upon the walls of Egyptian temples—dim, vague, fragmentary, yet giving us glimpses of insight and flashes of light,
which aid much in the understanding of the
meaning of to-day.   We find the instincts of
the race renewed in each new-born infant.
Each individual child desires to master his
surroundings.   He cannot yet drive a real
horse and wagon, but his very soul delights
in the three-inch horse and the gaily painted
wagon attached; he cannot tame real tigers

and lions, but his eyes dance with pleasure as
he places and replaces the animals of his toy
menagerie; he cannot at present run engines
or direct railways, but he can control for a
whole half-hour the movement of his miniature train; he is not yet ready for real father-
hood, but he can pet and play with, and rock
to sleep, and tenderly guard the doll baby.

Dr. Seguin also calls attention to the fact
that a handsomely dressed lady will be passed
by unnoticed by a child, whereas her counter-
part in a foot-long doll will call forth his most
rapt attention ; the one is too much for the
small brain, the other is just enough.

The boy who has a toy gun marches and drills
and camps and fights many a battle before the
real battle comes. The little girl who has a
toy stove plays at building a fire and putting
on a kettle long before these real responsibilities come to her.

A young mother, whose daughter had been
for some time in a Kindergarten, came to me
and said, "I have been surprised to see how
my little Katherine handles the baby, and how
sweetly and gently she talks to him." I
said to the daughter, "Katherine, where did
you learn how to talk to baby, and to take care
of one so nicely? " " Why, that's the way we

talk to the dolly at Kindergarten!" she replied. Her powers of baby-loving had been developed definitely by the toy-baby, so that when the real baby came, she was ready to transfer her tenderness to the larger sphere. Thus, as I said before, toys form a bridge between the great realities and possibilities of life, and the small capacities of the child. If wisely selected, they lead him on from conquering yet to conquer. Thus he enters ever widening and increasing fields of activity, until he stands as God intended he should stand, the master of all the elements and forces about him, until he can bid the solid earth, "Bring forth thy treasures;" until he can say unto the great ocean, "Thus far shalt thou go and no farther;" until he can call unto the quick lightning, "Speak thou my words across a continent;" until he can command the fierce fire, "Do thou my bidding;" and earth, and air, and fire, and water, become the servants of the divine intelligence which is within him.

CHAPTER IV.

THE INSTINCT OF LOVE, OR THE TRAINING OF THE AFFECTIONS.

With the first dawning smile upon the infant's face the instinct of love awakes. Until the last sacrifice of life itself for the loved object—aye, on up to that sublime exaltation which can say even though He slay me, yet will I trust Him, love is the great motive power which enriches and ennobles life. Can we, therefore, too carefully watch and train its first growth? In every stage of man's development, unselfish love plays a part; it is the basis of all contentment within one's own soul; of all happiness in the family life; of all friendship in the social world; of all patriotism in state affairs; of all philosophic understanding of the world-order; of all religious contemplation of God. Yet this instinct, so manifest in each infant as it holds out its loving arms to its father, or hides its face upon its mother's shoulder from the gaze of a stranger, does not always serve the purpose for which it has been assuredly given. Loving warm-hearted little children grow into cold, selfish men and women, and many a parent who has given his *all* to his children has to exclaim with Lear, "How sharper than a serpent's tooth it is to have a thankless child!"

Selfishness is the most universal of all sins, and the most hateful. Dante has placed Lucifer, the embodiment of selfishness, down below all other sinners in the dark pit of the Inferno, frozen in a sea of ice. Well did the poet know that this sin lay at the root of all others. Think, if you can, of one crime or vice which has not its origin in selfishness. Why is this? To one who has thoughtfully and carefully studied the subject, the cause of the widespread prevalance of selfishness is not hidden. It lies largely in the mother's non-apprehension of the right treatment of her child's *earliest* manifestations of love. As the instinctive activity of the child can descend into destruction or ascend into creativity ; as the undisciplined or disciplined exercise of the senses can degenerate into unbridled gratification of the passions, or can grow into moral control of all the life; as the spontaneous, imitative play of the child can fill his mind with weak and vicious examples to be copied, or inspire his life with high and noble ideals to be followed; as the inborn desire for recognition can develop into bragging vanity, or expand into reverent endeavor,—so too has the instinct of love its two-fold tendency. There is a physical love which expresses itself in the mere kiss, and hug, and word of endearment. This is not the all-purifying, all-glorious love, so elevating to every life; it is but the door, or entrance, to that other higher form of love which manifests itself in service and self-sacrifice.

The love which instinctively comes from a child to its mother is usually shown in the caressing touch of the baby hands, the tremendous hug of the little arms, the coaxing kiss of the rosy lips, and is to the fond mother an inexpressible delight. Nor need she rob herself of one such moment; while her child is in the loving mood, let her ask of him some little service, very slight at first, but enough to make him put forth an effort to aid her. Thus can she transform the mere selfish love of the child into the beginning of that spiritual love which Christ commended when he said, "If ye love me, keep my commandments." Let her remember that against the mere protestations of attachment, He also uttered those stern words of warning, "Not every one that saith unto me, Lord, Lord, shall enter into the kingdom of Heaven, but he that doeth the will of my Father which is in Heaven." The parent stands, for the time being, to his child as the one supreme source to whom he looks for all things; the center of all his tiny affections. The relationship established between parent and child is apt to become, in time, the relationship between the soul and its God. The thought is a solemn one, but a true one.

The earthly affections are the ladders by which the heart climbs to universal love. "*Love is to be tested always by its effect upon the will.*" The grace of God can turn the weak, selfish will from thoughts of self to thoughts of others, but it cannot make a life all that the life would have been, had that will from the beginning been made strong and unselfish by repeated acts of loving self-sacrifice, even in human relationship. Contrast for yourself the selfish, all-absorbing love of a Romeo and a Juliet who could not live if the physical presence of the loved one were taken away, with that grandly beautiful love of Hector for Andromache, who, out of the very love he bore her, could place her at one side and answer the stern call of duty, that she might never in her future memory of him have cause for painful blush. It has been one of the great privileges of my life to have had en-

trance to an almost ideal home, where husband
and wife were filled with the most exalted
love I have ever known. In time the husband
was called hence. The wife said: "All that
was beautiful or attractive in my life went out
with my husband, and yet I know that I must,
for the very love I bear him, remain and rear
our child as he would have him reared." As I
listened to these words, quietly uttered by the
courageous wife, I realized what love, real love,
could help the poor human heart to endure.

Froebel, believing so earnestly that it was
only by repeated training in many small acts
of self-sacrifice that the child attained unto
the right kind of love, would have the mother
begin with her babe in her arms, to play that
its wee fingers were weaving themselves into a
basket which was to be filled with imaginary
flowers to be presented to papa as a token of
baby's love. The motto intended for the
mother, in the little "Flower Basket" song,
says :

> "Seek to shape outwardly
> Whatever moves the heart of the child,
> Because even the child's love can decay
> If not nourished carefully."

A statement of the same truth in general
terms would be that the inward must always

find expression in the outward if it would have a healthful completeness. Especially is this true of any tender emotion or sentiment, which, unused, soon degenerates into mere sentimentality, becoming satisfied with itself as a delightful sensation, or, worse still, shrivels up into skepticism or cynical doubt as to the reality of any genuine emotion.

Froebel would show the mother what a mighty instrument in her hands such childish play can become, "and," says Madam Marenholtz von Bulow, "none but those who do not understand and observe the nature and character of children, who have forgotten their own childhood, will consider it a piece of far-fetched absurdity thus to interpret the earliest games of children as the starting-point of the life of the Soul, and the beginning of mental development." The mother's effort is in no wise to stop with the *playful* service of her child but by such plays she can incline him toward the desired line of conduct. She is to bear ever in mind the words of the beloved disciple, "He that loveth not his brother whom he hath seen, how can he love God whom he hath not seen?" That there might be no mistake as to the kind of brotherly love here referred to, the aged saint had already explained, "whoso hath this world's good, and seeth his brother have need, and shutteth up his bowels of compassion from him, how dwelleth the love of God in him?"

With the realization of the necessity of early and constant training that the great end may be attained, the mother is to exercise, in the little immortal, this divine kind of love, through his every-day contact with herself and his father, his brothers and sisters, in order that his effortless love may develop into the kind which can not die. Of all the essentials of true character-building, there is perhaps none more important than this, that the child should learn, *through love*, to give up his own will to others; for the sake of others should learn from the very beginning of life to submit to things which are unpleasant to him. It would not be difficult to make children obey, if this thought had been carried out from the beginning, before egotism, self-will and selfishness had gotten fast hold upon the young heart. "Again," says Madam Marenholtz, "all work, all exercises which awaken the active powers, which form the capacity for rendering loving service to fellow creatures, will help to lay the groundwork of religion in the child. The awakening of love goes before that of faith; he who does not love can not believe. Loving self-surrender

6

to what is higher than ourselves, to the Highest
of All, is the beginning of faith.   But love
must show itself in deeds, and this will be im-
possible unless there is a capacity for doing.
A child can no more be educated to a life of
religion and faith without the exercise of
personal activity than heroic deeds can be ac-
complished with words only."

Never should the mother, through that foolish
desire to keep her child as long as possible
dependent upon her, or that worse pride which
would show itself to be self-sufficient, refuse
the proffered help of her child.   If she is doing
something in which, from the nature of the
thing, he can not share, let her be careful to
substitute some other loving service while de-
clining the one proffered, remembering that
love, turned away, nourishes selfishness; and
p   help refused, begets idleness.   She
may have to say, "No, dear, you can not help
dress the baby;" she can add, " you may hand
mamma the clothes."   I know of one household
in which it is as much the self-imposed duty
of the child of three to patiently hold the towel
and soap, until needed, as it is the mother's
part to bathe the year-old brother.   In another
household in which the six-year old child had
long been taught that true love showed itself

in service rather than protestations, the mother was one day compelled by a severe headache to shut herself up in a darkened room. Her boy soon opened the door and asked her some question. "Mamma can not talk to you to-day, Philip, she has a headache. Go out and shut the door." The door was quietly closed, and in a few moments a mysterious bumping and rolling about of the furniture was heard in the next room. All was still for a short time. Then softly and gently the door was again opened, and little Philip stepped on tip-toe to his mother's bedside. "Mamma," said he, "I've straightened the furniture in the sitting-room all up so nicely, and fixed your work basket; isn't your headache better?" The loving little heart had prompted this difficult service in order that the love called forth by her suffering might find vent.

All birthdays, Christmas celebrations, and other festivals, can be made occasions for the uniting of the whole family in glad and loving service for the honored one, who in his turn may serve to an extra extent the others, *because* the honors of the day have been conferred upon him. In m   r Kindergartens, the child who is selected as leader for each day has also the office of distributing the work, gathering up the luncheon baskets, and otherwise waiting on the rest, that he may thereby gain the impression that *honors and responsibilities go hand in hand*, and begin to realize the meaning of the significant words, " He that is greatest among you shall be your servant." Mothers have scarcely realized the value of the family festival rightly kept, the opportunity it gives them for exercising the loving little hearts in unselfish love, more especially if they and the fathers enter into the childish secrets and mystery of preparation. Perhaps papa can come home half an hour earlier because it is Mildred's or Bradford's birthday, and mamma and Mildred and Bradford can plan some little surprise for papa before he gets there; it matters not how trifling, provided each has made an effort to complete it.

If, at the magic words, "Finish it for mamma and let it show her how much you love her," mothers could see the look of almost angelic delight upon the little faces when the discouraged hands have picked up the tangled sewing card, or have undone the wrongly woven mat, they would not so often rob themselves of this pleasure. This appeal to the spiritual love can, as I have already said, be made a means of the noblest form of government, that of voluntary, loving obedience. The childish heart responds quickly to such an appeal, as it does to all things noble and generous and beautiful. At one time I had in my Kindergarten a delicate, nervous child, who occupied the chair next to me in order that I might the more carefully guard him. One day he chanced to be absent, and a rosy little Scotch lad asked if he might not take the place. I consented. Next morning, little Jean, the frailer child, was again with us; but my sturdy young Scotchman was in the chair, and with the persistence of his race, refused to give it up, even holding on to my dress in his determined way. "Oscar," said I, "why do you want to sit next to me?" "Cause I love you so much," was his honest and emphatic reply. "Why," said I, i   tone of assumed surprise, "isn't your love strong enough to stretch across the table?" "Yes, it is," he answered, and at once left the contested seat and resumed his usual place at some distance from me. Each time during the morning that our eyes met, his shone with the light of this higher love ; he had made what, to him, was a sacrifice, to prove his devotion, and the added happiness was his also.

Children usually delight to be told that

their hands and feet and bodies can tell their love as well as their tongues. A little girl came to me one morning saying, "My hands loved you yesterday." "Did they?" I said. "Tell me about it." "Our baby tore my mat, and I was just going to slap her, but I thought of you, and I didn't." This explanation was given without the slightest thought of commendation for the self-control exercised, and was passed over by me as a thing of course in one of my children who really loved me. There is a story often told by kindergartners when they wish to establish this higher standard of love with a new set of children. It is of the Franciscan monks, who, in order that they might show their love for the Heavenly Father, left their homes and all the pleasant things about them, and spent their time in finding wanderers who had lost their way in the mountain's snow-storms, and in taking care of the sick, and in helping the poor, and in teaching the ignorant. From the very beginning they established a rule that the older monks should serve the younger and those who were strong should wait on the weak. I have never heard this story tenderly and attractively told, that it did not have an immediate effect upon the conduct of the older

children. One day, on perceiving signs of
selfishness among my children, I told it to
them, making no comment or application.
When I had finished, it was luncheon time.
As the napkins were being given out, one
rollicksome, usually thoughtless little fellow
exclaimed, "Oh, I do wish I could have that
pretty red and blue napkin to give to Bobby!"
"You can have it," said I. He took the napkin
and spread it out before his little cousin, who
was smaller than he. "I think," said a still
younger child, "*that's* the prettiest napkin in
the whole lot." "He can have it, can't he?"
asked little David. "You know he's so little."
Thus quickly had the spirit of the Franciscan
love taken possession of their young hearts.
There lies an almost untold wealth of resource
in the legends of the Roman Catholic saints,
nearly all of whom were canonized for their
deeds of self-sacrifice and service to humanity.
The Protestant church has robbed herself of
much, in shutting away from her children
these stories of pure, sweet lives, unto most of
whom it could have been said, "*Well done,*
thou good and faithful servant, enter thou into
the joy of thy Lord."

The "love-force," as another has called it,
is woman's greatest instrument of power.

Unmarred children implicitly believe that their mother's love makes everything easy. I have in my memory gallery a beautiful picture illustrating this perfect trust of the little child in the efficacy of his mother's love. Two little cousins of about three years of age are playing together on a green lawn, suggesting to the beholder white kittens in their free frolicsome gambols. One suddenly catches his foot in some unseen obstacle in his path and falls forward, striking his head against the trunk of a tree. Instantly, of course, there ensue loud cries of pain. The other little fellow is in a moment by his side, with his arm around him, and pushes him with all his might towards his own mother, saying as he does so, in the most assuring, coaxing tones possible, "Run to my mamma, Dean, run to my mamma, she'll kiss it and make it all well. *Please* run to her, *quick!*" Surely perfect love in this case has cast out all fear. Love engenders love. Can not this great God-gift of joyful self-sacrifice to the mother devise a thousand ways by which to kindle the same fire in her child, until the Robert Falconers of fiction are no longer beautiful dreams but living realities? "Ah," says the doubter, "what if I ask my child to do something for me, and he refuse, or begin

to make excuses, or ask why his brother or
sister can not do it as well?" You have simply
mistaken the time for stretching the young
soul's wings. Begin the training when the
child is in the loving mood, and you will
rarely fail to get the desired response. Yet,
if need be, command the performance of the
deed, that by repeated doing, the selfish heart
may learn the joy of unselfishness, and thus
enter upon *True living.*

"Let us strive to follow the ideal which our
Lord Himself has given to us, in all its ful-
ness in all its grand proportions. Let us aim
at nothing short of a life which will embrace
in it all the glory of the heavens, as well as
the gladness of the earth; which will put
'Thou,' 'Thine,' 'Thee,' in the first place,
'We,' 'Ours,' 'Us,' in the second."

CHAPTER V.

THE INSTINCT OF CONTINUITY, OR THE TRAINING
OF THE REASON.

What is it that gives the attraction to such rhymes as, "This is the house that Jack built?" Is it not that each step in this nursery tragedy is seen clearly to proceed out of the previous one and to develop into the succeeding one? What is it which makes the child ask at the end of a story, "What became of the little dog?" or, "What did the mamma say then?" Does not the question plainly show the child's dislike of *endings*, or *isolations?* Why do all children listen with delight to stories of when they were babies, or, better still, of when mamma was a little girl, or papa was a little boy it not that this gives to them the continuity of their little lives, or that of the parent's larger life? Have not the magic words "Once upon a time," "A long time ago," the same fascination for the very reason that they show him a connection with the remote past? How a boy's face lights up when one begins to talk with him about what he is going to do when he gets to be a man! The thought links him with the mysterious future. What is the attraction which the steady, never-stopping pendulum of the clock has for the child? It marks the continuity of time. Have you never soothed the restless fretting of a baby by call-ing his attention to running water or ·falling sand? This is the continuity of motion. " earliest cradles of the race were rocked in rhyme to sleep," sings the poet. It is the measured accentuation of sound in melody that has such charm for the child; all simple rhythmical measurement of music is a delight to him. Without doubt this is the secret charm in "Mother Goose" which has held enthralled generations of little listeners. So keen is the child's enjoyment of continuity in sound that he will take delight in running a stick along a picket fence, forming a kind of Chinese music in which his young soul rejoices, though older and more tired nerves may quiver thereat.

I remember once amusing myself and a small boy by drawing a picture of a wagon for him on a fragment of paper. He was interested and for a short time satisfied with it; then he returned with the request that a horse be drawn in front of the wagon. The scrap of paper did not admit of the drawing of a horse

in proper proportion to the wagon, so I care-
lessly drew the two hind legs and rear part of
the animal, and handed it back to him with
the remark, " We can't see the other part of
your horse; this will do." He looked at it for
a moment, then a great wave of disappointment
swept over his face and his lips quivered; in a
moment more he burst into tears. I was
astonished, and in the thoughtless impulse of
the moment, said, "If you are going to be a
naughty boy and cry I will not play with you."
This was before my kindergarten days. I
know now that the fragmentary picture gave a
sense of incompleteness to the sensitive little
brain, which was akin to the dissatisfaction and
unrest which come to us oftentimes when days
seem dark and dreary, and we cannot see the
continuity of the good steadfastly shining
beyond the temporary cloud of interrupted
plans or disappointed hopes. All these and
scores of like incidents are but indications of
the child's instinctive desire to get a better
comprehension of *process* or *continuity*.

Let us pause and think what is the true
significance of a realization of continuity. It
is one of the *central truths of life;* a comprehension of it is the mark of the philosophic
mind, of having attained unto that rationality

which brings insight. In fact, we have not
reached a really rational view of anything
until we see that all things are connected, *that
there is no such thing as isolation.* It has
been well said, " Most of the world is asleep
because it has been taught *facts* alone." It
has learned to see results without studying the
cause of these results; begin to show the living
moving process by which these results have
been obtained, and you begin to arouse the
sleeping world. The three-fold testimony of
nature, of history, and of revelation are not
wanting here.

Is it not the upheaval in primeval ages that
has formed our mountain ranges, which in their
turn determine the water courses? By these
pre-determined water courses which wash down
and grind up the fragments of rock, is not the
nature and productivity of the soil more or less
determined? Upon the richness or sterility of
the soil and the direction of the rain-bearing
winds, does not the nature of the vegetation
depend? Even the climate, that other great
factor in the physical world, depends somewhat
upon those primeval walls of rock. The insect
and animal life which any locality can sustain,
is closely connected with the vegetation and
climate; man's occupation or industrial activity

shapes itself according to the structure of the
surrounding country and the forms of vegetable and animal life about it; the influence of
those occupations is clearly seen upon the
mental bias of a nation, until at last the very
government of a people can be traced back to
the geography of the country.   In a thousand
and one ways nature illustrates this great
law of continuity.   The mist arises from the
ocean, ascends to the clouds, is floated across
the continent by the wind, comes in contact
with the cold mountain peak which changes it
into the form of rain, descends into rivulet and
stream, and is emptied by them back into the
ocean.   The trees grow centuries old and die;
their majestic forms crumble into loam which
serves to enrich the soil from which a new
growth of trees draws nourishment.   Even the
blood in the body is in a continual process,
from heart through artery and vein back to
heart again.   Our very gestures repeated
become attitudes, attitudes crystallize into
bearing, and bearing helps to mould character;
for may not one's bearing be an open gate
which invites all mankind to come in and sup
with us, or on the other hand may it not be the
iron portcullis which shuts out with like harsh-
ness the glorious knight who brings a message

from the king, or the trembling peasant who flees to us for help? Does not this joyous warmth and uniting sympathy on the one hand, and isolating unconcern of manner on the other hand, have much to do in their reaction with the formation of character?

We are all familiar with the principle in natural philosophy known as " the indestructibility of matter." We know that the accurate chemist can burn a piece of wood, and present us in smoke, gas and ashes every atom's weight of the wood; we know that in the processes of nature the elements of the earth change relationship but none are ever really lost. We see and acknowledge all this in *nature*, but we fail to realize it in human affairs. *It is because we fail to see continuity that we fail to comprehend life.* God is eternal, everlasting, ever present; therefore all His creation must reflect Him—*must be without isolations.*

In our modern civilization is every element of good for which Persian or Greek or Roman ever fought. The student of history with this thought of continuity in h mind, sees Providence bringing order out of chaos; sees the why and the wherefore of the terrible struggles through which the race has had to pass. The enormous sacrifice which any generation may

be called upon to make becomes a trifle when
the result of that slaughter and sacrifice is seen
in the next generation.   What was the battle
of Marathon, compared to the fact that upon
that battle-field the world gained the first
dawn of the gigantic truth that all men are
free?   What was the struggle of the Dutch
during their terrible thirty years war, compared
with the benefit which mankind has since
received from the firm establishment of the
fact that each soul shall be free to worship
God according to the dictates of his own conscience?   What were the sufferings of our
Puritan forefathers, compared to the protection
which a free government affords us, their
descendants, a protection bought by the very
courage and fortitude which their hard lot
engendered?   Continuity is the brightest lamp
of thought; by its light we see in Cæsar's
grasp of the Roman Empire the beginning of
modern civilization; in the Crusades, we find
the necessary preparation of the then narrowly
prejudiced nations for the future settlement of
America; by those fanatical wars were broken
down the fear of unknown countries, the small
provincial ideas of greatness, and the spirit of
adventure was aroused.   So, too, the true student of history traces back the French Revo-

lution far beyond the weak, vain rule of the
Louis to the desperate, profligate days of the
Popes, Julius II. and Leo X., which caused
the mighty soul of Michel Angelo to pour
itself out in pictures more terrible and sublime than any of which art had ever dreamed.
Then began the loosening of the hold of the
Roman Catholic Church upon the hearts of her
children, which finally resulted in the loss of
respect and reverence for everything that was
high or holy, for all forms of authority, in the
days of Murat and Robespierre.

In the affairs of to-day as well as in those of
past times we see this great law of continuity
explaining and making clear the vexing prob-
lems of the hour. By its magic touch, as by
the enchanted cloak of old, things assume their
right degree of importance. As for example,
in the rapid growth and advancement of the
railroads of our times can be plainly foreseen
the downfall of European aristocracy; by
means of these the arable lands of our great
Northwest, our prairie lands, are becoming the
granaries of the world, are helping to send
food to the heretofore dependent vassals of the
old world, whose bread had come to them only
by the consent of the lords of the land.

Great as is the insight that continuity gives

7

to the student of science or of history, greater still is its aid to the student of morals.   I once had a man of the world tell me that for the life of him he could not with any comfort go out fishing or upon any pleasure expedition on Sunday, because during his childhood his mother had so constantly and conscientiously put aside all secular occupations on that day. " Train up a child in the way he should go," says the Bible, the best book on pedagogics ever written, " and when he is old he will not depart from it;" when seeming departure from the standards acquired in early childhood comes, it can almost always be traced to inconsistencies in the training.   So, too, apparently sudden defalcations usually bring to light a train of previous actions which show to the observing eyes that the rottenness had been of long though hidden growth.

Froebel considered this such an important part of education, that he would have the mother begin to point it out to her child in such trifling matters as that of showing him in song or play that the bread and milk which have disappeared after his supper is over are yet existing in the form of fresh blood in him, serving to make his cheeks " red and white like

rose and cream." In the motto to the mother
in this little song of "All's Gone," he says:

> "The child, disturbed, thinks all is gone,
>   When the empty plate and cup he sees;
>   Thou canst a wiser thought make known
>   And easily his fancy please,
>   Since what has vanished from us here
>   Exists yet in another sphere.
>   What from the outer form is flown,
>   Will in another form be known."

The child sees only the empty bowl;—ending,
loss, disconnection, isolation, hence discord.
The mother knows that the bread and milk are
changed into the higher form of blood and
muscle ; instead of ending, she sees continua-
tion; instead of loss, gain; instead of discord,
perfect harmony.

Do we, when we look at the more complex
problem of life, see with the eyes of the child
or the mother? Do we see that all things work
together for good? It is into such a grand
view of life that the little child can be led as
naturally and as healthfully as into the realization that he breathes or that he has brothers
and sisters. In fact, that only is the right
education which makes all learning serve as an
instrument with which to train the child to see
in an effect the cause; in other words, to become
a rational being, to whom the great truths of

life have been shown. The question is, how shall we deal with the child so that he shall first feel this connection, then know it, then live it ? It is with this logical training in view, that the Kindergarten schools of sewing, weaving, and the like, are so arranged that one design grows out of another, though of course due attention is paid to the free, spontaneous growth of the child's own ideas. "See into what other pretty form you can *change* this one," says the teacher, or by some like remark suggesting orderly transformation rather than disconnected rearrangement, yet giving full scope to the child's individuality. The chairs, beds, tables, etc., built of the blocks, tablets, and sticks, are usually developed one from another, much to the delight of the children, thus giving an almost imperceptible tendency to see *transformation* rather than *mere change*. That this is the effect of logical play and work in any child who has gone through a thorough kindergarten, will be conceded by any observer.

In the kindergarten of a friend of mine a play with the blocks was going on, in which one form was thus changed into another by each move of the blocks. After several such changes had been made at the suggestion of the teacher, one little fellow looked up with the

most .astonished and delighted expression of
face, and exclaimed: " Well, I declare! It's
just too funny to see how one thing *busts*
into another without breaking up." Madam
Marenholtz von Bulow, the valued friend and
interpreter of Froebel, in speaking of this logical play, says: " He (the child in the kindergarten) is instructed in an easy manner how to
invent new forms at pleasure in endless variety
by application of Froebel's law of formation.
The forms and figures thus brought out, easily
proceed step by step to the most complex, only
appearing difficult and beyond the child's power
when we do not know how they *proceeded from
each other*. And again : " The child before
whose eyes sensible objects are brought in the
correct order of the parts to the whole, and in
the *logical* connection of things, will, when
reflected power is developed, also perceive this
order and logical connection clearly and definitely in the intellectual world."

In our legendary stories of heroes, we usually
begin to tell of them when they were little
boys, letting the children see the gradual
growth in character. My own children are
never tired of listening to such stories as that
of the little girl who wanted to make some
bread all by herself, so she was referred by

mamma to the cook, by the cook to the grocer
for flour, by the grocer to the miller, by the
miller to the farmer for wheat, by the farmer
to the ground, by the earth to the sunshine
and showers, and by these to the Heavenly
Father, who is back of all and in all. This
little story embodies much of the real significance and the comprehension of continuity.
It reveals the dependence of the individual
upon the rest of mankind, and also man's
dependence upon nature, and leads up to a
realization of the dependence of all upon the
Creator, which is the grand central truth of
religion.

The earnest mother can give a like logical
training in the home. Your child has bumped
his head; let him see that it was not the fault of
the table but of himself, because he did not
know where he was going; thus by learning
the cause, he learns to avoid further bumps.
He comes to you complaining of the stomach-
ache; sympathize with him, if need be, but ask
at the same time, "What has my child been eating which has made his stomach ache?" One
little fellow who had been trained, not only to
trace back physical aches, but irritated moods,
to disordered stomachs, was with me at a hotel
for a few days. He was much pleased by the

new experience of riding up and down in the elevator. One day he surprised me by saying, "I guess that elevator man has got all over his stomach-ache." "What!" I exclaimed. He gravely repeated his remark, and then added by way of explanation, "He was awful cross yesterday, and told me to keep out of the elevator, and to-day he offered to sharpen my pencil for me, and asked me to come and ride with him." Ah me, if dear old Carlyle could only have had that insight and have taken care of his diet while he was exposing and trying to correct the shams of society!

Two little girls in my kindergarten were once telling of a quarrel they had had the afternoon before with a playmate. One said: "When I got home, I told my mamma, and she said she wouldn't play with little girls who quarreled so, if she were in my place." Then turning to her companion she added, by way of confirmation of the justice of the decision, "So did your mamma, didn't she, Josephine?" "No," answered Josephine, in a low tone and coloring slightly. "My mamma said if I had been pleasant and unselfish we need not have quarreled." The first mother merely defended her child, laying the blame of the common fault elsewhere. The second mother carefully pointed out to her child the cause of the quarrel, not of that quarrel only but of all quarrels. One of the great benefits of logical training is that each new glimpse into cause and effect applies to all after like experiences.

We will have to give a separate chapter to logical punishments, so misunderstood is the subject, so beneficial the right line of conduct in the matter. The loving mother whose instinct has once been aroused into insight, will find innumerable ways by which to teach her child to see connection of one thing with another, and the child's desire for such connected views of things will suggest many more. In the family life, the loving anticipation of how pleased papa will be when some little piece of work is done, the planning beforehand for some excursion to the country, or the celebration of some birthday, leads the child to trace out the origin of unselfish happiness, and is worth ten-fold the joy which is obtained from impulse alone. Not that the spontaneous joy of a child is ever to be checked, only it can be made reasonable, and the child gradually learns to subordinate the gratification of the moment to a better though more distant enjoyment; a lesson much needed by the majority of mankind. In the spending of money, some

object can be placed before the child which
will have sufficient attraction for him to induce
him to save his pennies until enough are
acquired to purchase the desired article, rather
than that habit, thoughtlessly engendered in
most American homes, of expecting a child to
spend each cent, bestowed or earned, as soon as
he gets it. It is this wretched spendthrift propensity which shackles half the world,
and makes men slaves to their circumstances
rather than masters over them.

Even in the selection of reading matter for
children, this development of the power to
reason can be furthered. Such books as "Seven
Little Sisters" lead the young mind to see the
unity of the race, and such books as "Ten Little
Boys on the Road from Long Ago until Now"
lead him to trace in history the connection of
the civilization of the world.

In science work with the children a connection can be made between the *animal* kingdom
and the *mineral* kingdom, by following the
study of mollusks with that of shell rock, or
other fossiliferous rock; the *mineral* kingdom
can be connected with the *vegetable* kingdom
through mixing the clay and sand with the
vegetable loam, as together they form the food
of the plant-world which gives to man and the

lower animals nourishment. It is helpful to call the child's attention to such facts as these, that birds which live upon the smaller inhabitants of the water are so constructed that they can wade or swim ; that almost all weak creatures have the power of fleeing rapidly, and the added protection of having the color of their usual environment, thus showing design, hence connection in creation. All sympathy with the varying phases of the weather aids the child. The good rain is giving the flowers and grasses a drink, although it is keeping us indoors; the hot sun is making the corn grow and the fruits ripen, although it is uncomfortable for us; the soft snow and even the sharp frost are covering up the roots of trees and plants, and putting them to sleep for a new growth in the spring. Almost any child, no matter how willful, can be trained into logical rationality, if little by little, in a bright, cheery way, he is taught to look before and after.

In a visit to a friend not long ago, I had full opportunity to demonstrate how quickly a child responds to reason if the reason is simply enough put. Her little son, a beautiful boy of five, refused to eat any meat for breakfast. " Please eat a little, Harvey," said the mother. " No," responded the child. "Please do, for

mamma's sake." "No, I don't want any,"
almost petulantly replied the child. The mother
looked baffled and distressed. "Harvey," said
I, "do you know what the little stomach does
when it gets hold of some nice meat?" "No,"
said the child, interested. "Your little stomach, you know," continued I, "has to change
the food you send down to it into blood and
bone and muscle, so when it gets sugar and
cookies and things that taste nice to you
but do not help it to make strength, it twists
and turns them, and does the best it can with
them, but it cannot make very good blood with
them. But when you send it good strong meat,
it goes to work and grinds it up and makes it
into fine, rich blood, which is sent out into
your arms and legs and makes strong muscles,
so that you can climb trees and run fast and do
all sorts of things without getting tired." I
talked in an animated fashion as if these things
were the most desirable attainments in all life.
Harvey gradually drew his plate toward him
and began a vigorous attack upon the rejected
meat.

The tracing of faults in your children back
to the causes of them, helps much in rooting
them out. Everyone recognizes evil when it
culminates in some forbidden *deed*, but the

wise mother perceives that the act is but the result of a chain of previous evils. Let a child steal and you are horrified, but you do not perceive that this is only a climax; it began with secretiveness, then followed meddling with what belonged to another, then perhaps the covetous thought or the lack of some sort of ownership, finally ending in thievery—at any stage it could have been checked more easily than at the last. Too many mothers and teachers fail in the training of children because they do not recognize the law of continuity. I use the two words mother and teacher almost as if they were synonymous. They are as far as the training of the little child is concerned? The true mother is a teacher whether she is conscious of it or not, and the true teacher uses the innate mother element, that which broods over the child and warms it into life as much as she does her acquired knowledge. The full realization of the value of the first years of a child comes only when we perceive the continuity of character building. Not alone is the little child affected by having the connection of things shown to him, but unthinking adults, those children of a larger growth, too, feel the effects.

The young man just starting upon his business career sees the man of business who has accumulated capital and influence, and he is stirred with desire, or perchance with envy, and wishes in a vague way that he could be as "lucky." Show him the process by which the man made his fortune; if it be honestly won, how he denied himself luxuries in his early career, how he was prompt in meeting every engagement, reliable in every transaction, polite, courteous, and good-natured, though firm and unhesitating, and if you make the young aspirant after fortune see this you arouse him to do likewise, and earning a fortune becomes a real possible thing, not a gift of fate. Or if the fortune has not been accumulated by the legitimate process of business, but by wild and reckless speculation, the curse of our Nation, show him the inevit- able process; that as the bank account unjustly swells, so surely does the conscience and honor of the man shrink, until at last *money* has taken the place of *manhood*, and the younger man's desire for the ill-gotten gains changes into commiseration of the poor deluded soul which has robbed *itself* far more than it has robbed the world.

Or again, the young student, who discovers what books the philosopher has read or would recommend for reading, feels that he has obtained possession of a ladder by which he too may climb to the dizzy height of scholarship attained; it becomes a stimulus to his flagging energies. It is this realization of *inevitable process* in all success that does away with that fatal paralysis of effort, a belief in good or bad luck, with which many a young man satisfies his conscience or smothers his aspirations. Let him from childhood be led to realize that there is no *luck* about it, but that each man makes or mars his own fortune, and if there remains a spark of the ideal in him it kindles into flame. Many of the questionings of the human heart as to the justice of Divine dealings can be satisfied by the light of this law.

> " I sent my Soul through the invisible,
>   Some letters of the after-life to spell;
>   And by and by my Soul returned to me,
>   And answered, 'I myself am Heaven or Hell'."

Hell thus becomes "God's highest tribute to man's freedom."

In a thousand ways we can test the importance or non-importance of any line of progress. Out of what has it grown? Into what is it leading? All events in time are links in a chain. The human race is one continued

whole, each child is the heir of generations
unnumbered. "Hereditary rank," says Washington Irving, "may be a snare and a delusion,
but hereditary virtue is a patent of innate
nobility which far outshines the blazonry of
heraldry." In each of our own lives is to be
seen at work this great law. "We are to-day
what we are because our past has been what it
was; what we will be in the future depends
upon what we now are." Nor is this all. We
are now, by our voluntary choosing of this or
that line of conduct, forming character and
creating spiritual tendencies which shall be
transmitted to our descendants; thus we are
linked not alone with the past, but with the
future. Is not this thought an inspiring one
to every mother? By every weakness which
she helps her child to overcome, by every
inspiration which she fans into flame, is she
upbuilding not only her child's character, but
is benefiting all after generations. What
confidence it gives her, too, as to her child's
future. He must go out into the world and
fight his battles alone; but she can arm him
with the armor of good habits, place upon his
head the helmet of rational self-determination,
put into his hand the sword of aspiration, and
above all, give to him the shield of faith and

reverence, so that he goes forth ready to defy the demons of appetite within and the devils of temptation without. She need not fear to send her son forth, or tremble for her daughter's happiness—they have begun aright and the law of continuity will keep them aright, unless some mighty force hurl them for a moment from the path of rectitude, and even then the reaction will swing them back into the accustomed path.

Is more evidence needed to impress upon the mother's heart the importance of training her child to feel and see continuity in all things around him—in all he does?

CHAPTER VI.

THE INSTINCT OF JUSTICE, OR RIGHT AND WRONG PUNISHMENTS.

One morning last year, I went over to one of our kindergartens located in a sad part of the city, only a few blocks away from the residence portion where wealth and culture abound. It was composed of the neglected children of the dissipated and rather dissolute poor. We had recently put a young girl in charge of them, and I was anxious to see how she was getting on. To the practiced eye of a trained kindergartner, the handwork of each child tells his mental and moral condition. The children at the table where the young director was seated were at work on second gift beads, stringing cubes and balls by twos. All seemed to be interested and busy at their little task except one child, whose string showed no system, definiteness, or harmony; orange, green, purple, yellow, balls, cubes, and cylinders, were strung at random. The jarring inharmony in color and the disorder in form showed the discord within. On the cheeks of the young director were two bright spots of color, though she appeared calm and quiet. When the work-time had ended, she asked the children if they would not like to have their beads hung up to help make the room pretty for the other children. String after string was taken up, and the delighted little workers watched her wind them around the gas-fixtures. At length she came to the disordered string before mentioned. " Ah," said she quietly, " I am sorry Nellie's string is not nice enough to hang up. She will have to wait until she can learn to string her beads in some pretty fashion before we can hang them up for her." Instantly the child threw the string of beads petulantly upon the table, and the look of sullen defiance deepened in her face. The young teacher walked to the piano and struck the chords which were a signal for all to rise from their seats. All arose but Nellie. The second chord called them into position, and to the measured time of the music they marched forward and formed in a line upon the play-circle. The kindergartner then went over to the children, saying as she passed the chair of the obstinate Nellie, " Are you not coming to join with us in the Good-bye song ? " " No," exclaimed the child passionately, " *I shan't come.* If you break every bone in my body, I won't stir from this spot," and the look of

sullenness deepened into an almost fiendish expression. The color increased in the face of
the young kindergartner, but her voice was as
clear and as smooth as ever as she replied, "I
do not intend to hurt you, Nellie. When you
feel like doing what is right, you may come
and tell me." Then the Good-bye song was
sung and the good-bye shake of the hand was
given to each child, and all were dismissed to
their homes. Not another word was said, but
the young teacher sat down at a table and began
straightening out the mats and piling up the
work, preparatory to putting it away. Her face
was calm and serene, and save for the telltale
color of the cheeks one could detect no excitement or annoyance on her part. The tick of
the clock was the only sound heard in the
room. In a few moments the child gave an
uneasy jerk of her chair. "Are you ready,
Nellie?" asked the teacher, without looking
up. "No," answered the child emphatically.
The girl went on with her work. After a time—
I think not more than ten minutes—the child,
feeling the isolation of her condition, and
seeing that she would gain nothing by continued
obstinacy, arose hesitatingly from her chair and
sidled, in a half-indignant, half-sullen sort of a
way, up to the kindergartner. Although the

child's dress was greasy and torn, the young girl put her arm around her and drew her close to her, saying gently, " Well, Nellie, are we going to be friends? " Nellie seemed ready to burst into tears, and put her hand tremblingly upon the teacher's shoulder. Nothing was said in the way of reproof. After a minute the kindergartner said in a cheerful tone, " Do you think we can start all new to-morrow morning, Nellie? " and the child nodded her assent.

I have told this story simply to show what self-control can be obtained in such trying moments, through the *insight* which comes from a knowledge of the *true office* of punishment. To the misapprehension of the *aim* of punishment is due much of the misgovernment of children. Until a man has become a law unto himself, he is of no great value to the rest of the world; and *punishments, rightly considered, are not merely an atonement for offences committed,* but they *show the nature of the offence,* and help the individual to build up the law within and thereby to avoid repeating the misdeed. The child must be led from the unconscious to the conscious choosing of such lines of conduct as he is to pursue. How can he thus choose unless he knows these lines of conduct definitely, and thus can voluntarily decide which he will adopt? The deed is best known through its consequences. "By their fruits ye shall know them," says the Bible. Therefore we rob our children of one of the greatest aids to self-government and self-control, when by any means whatsoever we free them from the consequences of their own wrong-doing. That the child should early learn that "the way of the transgressor is hard," is an important part of his education. Could the souls just entering upon a career of dissipation, dissoluteness, or other form of vice, clearly see the end from the beginning, surely most of them would be deterred from pursuing the path of sin. But the fatal thought, "Somehow *I'll* escape," blinds many who have not learned the great law of continuity, who do not realize that "he who sows the wind *must* reap the whirlwind." As the germ of the plant can be seen in the tiny seed, as the germ of the future man is found in the little child, so too can the germ of the *inevitable consequences* be perceived in the deed. Thus we recognize the value of training the child by means of *retributive* punishment rather than by the *arbitrary* punishment too often used with children. The former appeals to the child's inborn instinct of justice. If he is led to feel that the inconvenience, discomfort, pain, or disgrace, is merely the natural consequence of his deed, as a rule he accepts it without rebellion or a revengeful thought. It is in this way that Nature teaches her laws to each child. The little one puts his hand upon the hot stove; no whirlwind from without rushes in and pushes the hand away from the stove, then with loud and vengeful blasts scolds him for his heedlessness or wrong doing. He simply is burned—the natural consequence of his own deed; and the fire quietly glows on, regardless of the pain which he is suffering. If again he transgresses the law, again he is burned as quietly as before, with no expostulation, threat, or warning. He quickly learns the lesson and avoids the fire thereafter, bearing no grudge against it. This is always Nature's method; the deed brings its own result, and nowhere is arbitrary unconnected punishment inflicted.

In history, we find this same law most effect-ually at work. The nations which violate the laws of progress and growth, and of interna-tional kindliness of feeling, suffer the conse-quences in the reaction upon themselves. Herodotus shows us that the Persian empire conquered and tried to *crush* the barbarians by whom it was surrounded, but in the end it was crushed by these same brutally-treated provinces. The Greeks colonized and civilized their border-lands, and in turn learned many useful things from them. The downfall of every great empire can be traced to its violation of the laws of justice and right in its dealings with surrounding nations. And that great law by which the deed returns upon the doer's head is thus written upon walls of adamant by the hand of time. We see how effectual retributive punishment, or rather retributive *justice*, works in the civic world. The business man who peremptorily discharges a clerk upon the first offence of drunkenness, has sober employees about him. The most successful business men will tell you that they do not dally with inefficiency. If an employee can do his work satisfactorily, he is kept; if he does it poorly, he is dismissed. Do we not see this same law in operation in society? Let an individual fail in the courtesies of society, and he is dropped by well-bred people, as the inevitable consequence of being boorish, rude, and discourteous. From sacred lips came the words, "With what measure ye mete, it shall be measured to you again." Can not the mother learn a great and needed lesson from all these sources? Can she not, in a thousand and one ways, serenely and calmly teach her child this

great lesson of life—that *no sin or wrong-doing
can be committed that does not bring its own
punishment ?* The more she lets the deed do
its own punishing, the more impersonal her
own part in the affair, the sooner does the
child learn the lesson.

Let me illustrate again. One morning we
had a box of sticks upon the table. A restless,
nervous little girl sat near it, and in a moment
or two put her hand into the box; as it was
near the edge of the table, I cautioned her
concerning it. Soon the little hand went in
again; the box tilted, slipped, and fell upon the
floor, while the sticks were scattered in a
hundred different directions. The child looked
u   startled manner. "What a time our
little girl will have picking her sticks up!" I
said, in a matter-of-course tone; "but I think
you can get through in time for the play circle.
Alvin, please move your chair so that she can
get the sticks which are under it." In a
moment the child was on her knees, rapidly
picking up the scattered sticks without a word
of objection or a murmur. Had I censured her,
or imposed some arbitrary punishment upon
her, I should in all probability have created a
spirit of rebellion, and have alienated her from
me, as she was a capricious and somewhat self-

willed child. As it was, *she* had upset the box,
and as a consequence *she* must pick up the
sticks. I have rarely ever failed in leading a
child to see the justice of such commands. In
fact, in a short time they usually take upon
themselves the rectifying of the mistake or
misdeed as they best can.

A little five-year-old boy one morning asked
the privilege of going into the next room and
refilling the water pitcher for us. It was
granted, as we always accept proffered services
when possible. Upon his return to the kindergarten I noticed some very suspicious looking
drops upon the mouth of the pitcher. "John,
did you spill the water?" I asked. "Just a
little bit," was the reply. "Get the sponge,"
said I, "and wipe it up quickly. We must
not ask anyone else to wipe up the water we
spill." In a few minutes he returned to the
room, and coming up to me with a somewhat troubled face, said in a puzzled manner,
as pondering the matter, "I guess those big
girls haven't got any sense." "Why?" I
asked. "'Cause they laughed when they saw
me wiping up the water I had spilled, so I
guess they haven't got any sense, or they
wouldn't laugh at a thing of that sort, would
they?" His sense of justice had so acquiesced

in the command that it seemed irrational to
him that anyone should be amused by the deed.

The mother, more than the teacher, has
opportunities to quietly let the deed impress
its nature upon the child's mind. Little children are naturally logical and quickly perceive
justice or injustice. The child who is rightly
treated will accept this right kind of punishment as a matter of course. A friend of mine
who had been given this idea of punishment,
upon returning home one day found that her
six-year-old boy had taken his younger brother
over to the wagon-shop across the street, a forbidden spot, and they had smeared their aprons
with the wagon-grease. In telling the story
afterwards, she said, "My first impulse was to
whip the boy, because he knew better than to
go; but I thought I would try the other way of
punishing him, and see if it would do any
good. So I said, 'Why, that's too bad. It will
be rather hard for you to get the grease off,
but I think I can help you, if you will get
some turpentine. Run to the drug store on the
corner and buy a small bottle of it.' " On his
return she took the two aprons and spread
them upon the floor of the back porch, then,
giving him a little sponge and the bottle of
turpentine, she showed him how to begin his

cleaning. In a few minutes he said, "Oh, mamma, this stuff smells horrid!" "Yes," she serenely replied, "I know it does; I dislike the smell of turpentine very much, but I think you will get through soon." So Willie kept on scrubbing until he had cleaned the aprons as well as he could. "Well," said his mother, as she helped him put away the cleaning material, "I think my boy will be more careful about going to the wagon shop, will he not?" "You *bet* I will!" was his emphatic reply.

A young mother who was filled with the spirit of the kindergarten, and had wisely guided her own children by the insight obtained from her kindergarten study, was called upon one summer to take charge of a little niece for a few weeks. The first morning after her arrival at her sister's home, she heard some angry words in the child's bedroom. On opening the door to inquire what was the matter, the nurse said, "Oh, it is just the usual fuss Miss Anna makes each morning over having to be dressed. I am sometimes an hour at it." Further inquiry showed that various means—such as bribing, coaxing, and threatening—had been used; but all to no avail. Even the last device used—that of depriving her of marmalade, her favorite dish, at each breakfast at

which she was late—had proved ineffectual.
The next morning the aunt went into the room
and said quietly, " Anna, you can have Mary
for twenty minutes to dress you; after that
time I shall need her down-stairs." The child
looked at her for a moment in astonishment
then went on with her play. In vain poor Mary
coaxed and urged. The twenty minutes
elapsed; the child was but half dressed. True
to her word, the aunt sent for Mary to come
down-stairs. "But, Auntie," called the child,
"I am not dressed yet." "Is that so?" said
the aunt. "I am sorry; jump back into bed
and wait until Mary comes again." In
about fifteen minutes the child called out
petulantly, "Auntie, I want to get dressed, I
tell you. Send Mary up to me." "I cannot
yet," replied the aunt from below; "she is busy
just now. Get into bed again, and she will
come as soon as she can." Breakfast was sent
up to the child by another servant. At the end
of an hour Mary came back, and it is needless
to say that little Miss Anna was quickly
dressed. The next morning the aunt again
gave the warning that Mary would be needed
down-stairs in just twenty minutes. This time
the warning took effect, and when Mary was
called the child was ready. The following

morning, the force of habit was too strong, and again came the capricious delay. Again Mary was called, and again the child was detained in her room for an hour. Two or three such experiences, however, were sufficient to break up entirely her habit of dallying. So quickly comes the lesson taught by retributive punishment. Many illustrations of the effectiveness of this method might be given, but surely are not needed by the thinking mind.

Another great advantage gained is, that retributive punishment is never inflicted in anger. Dante very graphically pictures angry souls as in a muddy, miry place, with a slow, foul mist about them, which hinders them from seeing clearly. If we turn to the nations of the world, we see upon a large scale the effects of the two ways of dealing with offenders. Among the Chinese it is customary, when any official has committed an offence against the law, to have him taken to the public square and whipped. What are the consequences of such treatment? Lack of self-respect, of self-reliance, and of self-government. In Great Britain and America, where the laws in general are but the instruments for meting out to each man the after-effects of his own deed, we see the growth of manliness, of self-government;

and of self-respect. Of course the question
will arise, "But what are we to do when the
logical punishment or consequence of a child's
deed will bring physical disaster?" In such
cases the moral disapproval of a mother should
be made strong and emphatic; if she has kept
her child in close sympathy with her, this will
be sufficient. On the other hand, scolding,
shaking, whipping, shutting up in dark closets,
and various other methods of arbitrary punishment, which have no possible connection in the
child's mind with the deed, are apt to rouse in
him a sense of injustice, and a feeling that the
parent has taken advantage of her greater
physical strength. By such treatment is also
violated one of the finest instincts of the child,
which is that of expecting justice, *absolute*
justice, from his parent. His sense of freedom
of conduct is injured, and, as I have said
before, he is robbed of one of the greatest
lessons of life, namely, *that each violation of
law, physical, mental, or moral, must be paid for.*
Learn to distinguish between mere overflow of
animal spirits and intentional wrong-doing; for
instance, do not punish your children for such
offences as having torn the finery with which
you have injudiciously clothed them, nor for

the accidents which may arise during a good-natured romp.

Of course too great temptations to commit a wrong deed must be avoided. There once came to me a mother with a face full of suppressed suffering. "What shall I do?" said she. "I have discovered that my boy steals money from his father's purse and from mine." "Give him a purse of his own," I answered, "and give him ways of earning money of his own; let a respect on your part be shown for his possessions, and thereby generate a respect on his part for your possessions. The superintendent of a reform school once told me that two-thirds of the boys who came to him were sent on account of having stolen, and that he always gave them, as soon as possible, a plat of ground which should be their own, and allowed them to raise their own vegetables, small fruit, or poultry, for the nearest market, in order that he might develop in them a sense of ownership, the lack of which he firmly believed was the cause of their transgressions." The mother left me somewhat comforted. A week or two after, she returned and said, "I have done as you advised, and the plan worked admirably; but this morning I went to the top drawer in my bureau to get my purse, and discovered that he had again been taking money from it." Here was an instance where, by leaving her purse within reach, the carelessness of the mother had placed in her child's way a temptation greater than he could resist.

Another advantage of the retributive method of punishment is that each deed is punished or rewarded upon its own plane. That is, material defeats or conquests bring material loss or gain, and spiritual defeats or conquests bring spiritual suffering or reward. Whereas, when this logical method of procedure is not followed, when a mere arbitrary punishment is substituted, the mistake is often made of rewarding or punishing spiritual efforts with material loss or gain, thereby degrading and lowering such efforts in the child's eyes. Many a mother thoughtlessly says to her child, " Be good to little brother while I am gone, and I will buy you some candy." "Give that to little sister, and I will give you something better." Self-control must not, in this way, be connected in the child's mind with gratification of physical appetite, nor can the child learn the sweet joy of unselfishness through the feeding of his greed of possession. I once discovered that a little girl in a primary class had written her spelling lesson upon the wrong side of the hem

of her linen apron. Upon my afterwards showing her the dishonesty of the deed, she burst
into tears and sobbed out, "I couldn't help it;
I couldn't help it. Papa promised me a
diamond ring if I wouldn't miss in my spelling
this year." The desire to obtain the coveted
jewel was so great that the bounds of honesty
and integrity had been overstepped. I once
knew a Sunday-school superintendent to say,
"Every boy who comes early for a month shall
have a present." Doubtless, punctuality was
obtained, but at the price of moral degradation.
Another illustration, an incident which hap-
pened in the childhood of a woman, shall be
told in her own words: "Once when I was a
little girl," she said, "our parents had left my
older sister and myself alone for the evening.
Getting sleepy, we went into our mother's
bedroom, and climbing upon the bed drew a
shawl over us, preparatory to a nap before their
return. In a little while my sister complained
of feeling cold. With the loving impulse of a
generous child, I gave her my part of the
shawl; with a real pleasure I spread it over
her, and we were soon asleep. Upon the return
of our parents, the question was asked why my
sister had all the covering while I had none.
Innocently enough, explanation was made in

9

the words, 'She was colder than I, so I gave
her my part.' 'You dear, blessed, unselfish
little thing!' exclaimed my father, 'here's ten
cents for you to reward you for your unselfishness.' A few evenings after, our parents were
again invited out, and again we children were
left alone in our part of the house. I began at
once planning a scheme to coax my sister to
again go into our mother's bedroom for a nap,
in order that I might repeat the deed which had
earned me ten cents. I succeeded, although this
time it was with some coaxing that I got her to
accept the extra portion of the covering. For
nearly an hour I lay waiting for the return of
my father, in order that I might gain financial
profit by my conduct." Thus easily and
quickly the sweet, generous, unselfish impulse
of a childish heart was changed by the mere
thought of material gain into sordid, selfish
and deceptive conduct.

When the mother realizes the true nature of
punishment, there is never detected in the
tones of her voice what Emerson calls a *lust of
power*. Too often children hear beneath the
mere word of command the undertone which
says, "I'll show *you* that I'll have *my way*."
The farther the child's self-government is
advanced, the higher his ideals of right and

wrong, the more will he resent this assertion of your personal will-power. If possible, let the instinct of justice, which is within each child, feel that the command has been given because the thing to be done is necessary and right. A child readily realizes that scattered toys must be gathered up, that soiled clothes must be changed, that tardiness necessarily brings a loss of opportunity, that money foolishly spent by him will not be re-supplied by the parent, that teasing or tormenting the younger brother or sister cause a loss of the society of the mistreated one, that petulance upon his part brings silence upon the part of the mother, that recklessness when on the street causes loss of liberty. When the punishments thus fall upon the plane of the deed in these minor offences, the child sooner learns to recognize the loss of respect which comes from lying, the dissatisfaction of ill-gotten gains, the weariness of hypocrisy, the wretchedness of jealousy, the bitterness of envy, the isolation of selfishness; he sooner learns that contentment comes only with honest gains, that respect follows always the upright man, that love springs up around the sympathetic soul, that happy participation is the reward of the unenvious, and that joy fills the unselfish heart.

I was walking one day with a young mother whose heart was filled with wild rebellion over the death of her beautiful baby. "Do not talk to me," she said, "of the justice or love of a God who could take from me such joy and cause me to suffer so much. I can not believe in such a Being." Just at this time we came upon her little daughter, about five years of age, who was playing in the street. "My dear child," exclaimed the mother, "run into the house at once. You will catch a severe cold out here. The wind is very sharp, and you are not sufficiently wrapped." "Oh, no, mamma," exclaimed the little girl, "I shall not take cold. Please let me stay." "My dear," said her mother sternly, "we will not argue the question; mamma knows best. Go into the house at once." As the child turned to obey the command, she burst into a flood of tears, and sobbed, "You do not love me, mamma. You do not love me, or you would not take my happy times away from me. You do not love me at all. I know you do not." We walked on in silence for some time. Suddenly my friend turned to me and said, "Why do you not tell me that my own child has answered my question?"

"Remain thou in the unity of life thyself,"

says Froebel, "or else thou *canst not* lead thy
child therein." We are not ready to teach our
children the true office and nature of punishment or retribution, until we ourselves perceive
that the sorrow and suffering which come to
us are but angels in disguise; until we are
ready to say with such grand souls as William
Gannett: "Though the heart cries, 'Is there
no *waste* of suffering?' when Nature burns
three hundred lives as readily as three, when
earthquake waves drown men like flies, when
the ignorance or sin of one man involves a
lineage or a nation in disaster, is there nothing
spendthrift in such tragedy? Again the mind,
slow-thinking, answers: That seeming spendthrift unconcern of Nature may be her deep
concern, that seeming waste may be some arch-
economy of tragedy. For see: to reach her
end—a 'man,' an ever-growing 'man'—as
speedily as possible, all fragments of experience
must be garnered up and utilized. To this end
are we bound together in one vast brotherhood
of acting and re-acting influences, all members
of the race, yea, of all races, actively and pas-
sively co-operating—nothing living, nothing
dying, to itself. That not a pang be lost, life
is linked to life across all time, across all space.
Linked in *time:* hence those dread laws of

heritage by which the crooked back and the disease are transmitted to irresponsible and helpless sufferers. That looks like waste of woe. At last they teach the world the rule of health; and clearing blood, the bones set straight, the lengthening average of life, the greatening powers of human joy and human usefulness,—all these transmitted also attest the good intent that lurked along the ages. And linked in *space:* the tiger cholera, stealing from the Ganges, strides with silent footfall through the nations, leaving death behind it, and at last robs homes upon the Mississippi's banks; the war in America starved English weavers and made the fields of Egypt white with cotton harvests. It looks like waste, but these are the 'vicarious atonements' of history, the great give-and-take by which the generations and the races bequeath and share experience, one suffering from and for another, to the end that 'man' may have life and have it more speedily and more abundantly. And there are countless small vicarious atonements of daily life, in which we all unceasingly take part—the everspread communion-table of the heart-break and the blood. It *is* tragedy. 'How long, O Lord!' we cry, as we gaze at the lasting, circling woe. But we can see that this communion *hives experience the faster*, and so *brings faster on the general good;* that by the same laws of communion, wisdom and saintship, also, are garnered in ministries of joy; that only by such co-operation, making the race one man, could life so soon have become the boon it is, the ever-richening boon it will be for future populations that will call us ancient. Not that we can always trace the vicarious and co-operative suffering to its outcome in beneficence; too vast and secret and complex are the connections in the social organism. But when, over and over again, evil is seen to be at last evolving good, assurance grows in us that good will always and everywhere prevail; and that the seeming exceptions will, when truly understood, prove subtler, vaster instances of the fact that the world's disorder is order-in-the-making."

If by your training you can give to your child this exalted view of life, is it not worth the self-control on your part which it requires?

CHAPTER VII.

INSTINCT OF RECOGNITION, OR THE TRAINING OF THE WILL.

"Must I do it?" exclaims the child, when he is confronted by the command of another, and the instinct of freedom begins to stir within him. "*Must* I do it?" This is an important period in each child's life, and should be well understood by the mother or teacher. How is the *obedience to the everlasting and eternal right* to be obtained, and yet, at the same time, the child be left to obey of his own accord? The problem is as old as recorded time, yet ever new, and demands a practical solution each day. In other words, by what process of training can the outward *must* be changed to the inward *ought*, and thus the child be developed into a free, self-determining being? "Unless a man has a will within him," says Emerson, "you can tie him to nothing." There is no wall or safeguard which love can build around its object strong enough and high enough to keep away temptation. The wall must be within, or else sooner or later the citadel yields to the enemy. One of

the most significant of the old Homeric stories
is that of the Greeks vainly endeavoring to build
up a wall in front of their ships which should
defend them from their Trojan foes, and thus
take the place of the strength and courage of
their hero, Achilles, who had withdrawn from
their midst. The moment of danger came; at
the height of the battle the wall gave way and
Hector and his troops rushed in upon them.
The same is true to-day that was true in the
days of the Iliad. Sooner or later external
walls must give way; the inner wall alone can
stem the tide of temptation. The moral will-
power of the child becomes strong only as his
conscience becomes enlightened and educated.

Whether the moral faculty is innate or a
matter of education, is a disputed point. "Inherited virtue," says Washington Irving, "is
a patent of innate nobility which far outshines
the blazonry of heraldry." It was President
Dwight, I think, who said that each child
should begin his education by selecting the
right kind of parents. Much can and should
be said upon the matter of the moral responsi-
bility which marriage brings. But granting
all that is urged concerning the inheritance
received from parents, we must still acknowledge that much is to be done in the training

of the will, and that far-reaching is the effect of its strength or weakness. Therefore the problem resolves itself into the question, how shall we educate aright the consciences of the children? Susan Blow has defined conscience as "a perception of what we are, in the light of what we ought to be." In the past, two methods of educating the conscience have been used. The first is that of requiring formal obedience. The intense desire to have the right thing done, created in the parent a sternness which compelled the child to obey, regardless of the fact that his rationality and will-power were thereby weakened, or rather not strengthened, and the parent's will often grew into tyranny. The will, like every muscle, organ, or faculty, becomes strong by being judiciously exercised. These advocates of formal, unhesitating, unquestioning obedience, frequently defend their position with quotations from Scripture; for example, they will cite you the words, "Spare the rod and spoil the child," utterly ignoring the fact that *rod* here means *punishment*, just as much as the word *pulpit* stands for *clergymen* in the sentence, "The pulpits endorse the movement," or the word *sail* for *vessel*, in "They captured ten sail." Again, they will frequently refer you to that passage of Scripture which says, "Children obey your parents," though they oftentimes forget to add, "in the Lord." We grant that the mere habit of doing right is something; with very small children, it is much. But the will, that safeguard in the hour of temptation, does not begin to grow until definite choice is made by the individual. Power to choose the right comes only from having chosen to do right many times. Oftentimes too great dependence upon the parent's will leaves the youth who has reached the age of maturity still a child in strength of will. This is, to me, the explanation why so many boys who have been strictly brought up by pains-taking, conscientious parents, suddenly enter upon a wild and reckless career as soon as they merge into the world at large.

The second method of educating the conscience is fully as detrimental. Many persons have realized that virtue, to be virtue, must be voluntary; that will-power, to amount to anything, must be the will-power which is within and not without the individual; they have therefore gone to the other extreme, and have required no obedience from the child, allowing his own caprice and the humor of the moment to govern him during that period of life when impulses are strong and rationality is feeble. This of course has been the extreme rebound from the severity of the first method. Words are scarcely needed to show the lack of wisdom in the parent or teacher who yields his judgment, which years of experience and observation and thought have matured, to the caprice of the child. I once asked a mother if her child was in any kindergarten. "No," she answered, "I took him to one, but he didn't care to stay, so I let him come home, and we have not attempted it since. I am sorry." The momentary mood of the child had over-ruled the rational judgment of the mother. Compulsion is the attempt to secure obedience regardless of the child's desire; this desire must appear before each right exercise of the will. Caprice is allowing the desire of the moment to govern the conduct, regardless of future consequences; whereas *voluntary obedience* is the deed which is performed after the right stages of will-growth have been passed through. First, the individual is led to desire to do a thing; second, he thinks about it; third, he wills to do it; and fourth, he voluntarily does it. Compulsion is the attempt to obtain the fruit of voluntary doing without the planting of the right seed. The creating of the desires for right conduct makes all the difference between *voluntary* and *forced* obedience. Unfortunate indeed is the poor little creature who is brought up without the idea of obedience. Bitter must be the lessons which experience will have to teach him if he ever truly masters his life. Too many children, who have never been given this idea of true obedience during childhood, make failures of their after careers from the simple fact that they have not learned that there are certain mighty laws which *must be obeyed.* I firmly believe, however, that most children when rightly trained can be *brought* into obedience without being *forced* into it.

There are of course many little devices which will aid the mother in leading her child to voluntarily do the right thing. For example, a strong-willed child—that is, a child with the instinct of freedom largely developed within him—can frequently be brought into the right way of doing by having a choice between two things given him. As, for example, "You may be quiet, or you must leave the parlor; you may pick up your playthings, or you must go without them to-morrow." Thus a certain amount of freedom is given to him by this opportunity to choose, and at the same time a

certain amount of obedience is exacted in that
he must choose one or the other of the alterna-
tives.   Again, a regular time is a great aid in
the performance of a duty.   The little one who
knows that at half-past seven he must go to
bed, is not apt to demur when the time comes;
whereas, the child who is sent to bed at seven
o'clock one night, at half-past seven another,
and at eight a third, is very apt to feel that the
bed hour is a mere whim on his mother's part,
and the inviolability of law which aided the
mother in the first instance is lacking in the
second.   A friend once sent her twelve-year-
old boy away from the table to wash his hands.
Upon his return, she said, "Will, why do you
persistently come to the table without washing
your hands, when you know that each time you
do it I send you away?"   "No," answered
the boy frankly, "you forgot to do it one time."
That one break in the continuity of command
had created in his mind the hope that he might
again escape the disagreeable duty.   Another
device is giving a child a definite time when he
must stop his play or work, with the assurance
that he can again begin it; as, for example,
"Come in now, it is time for you to practice;
you can go out again to-morrow," or, "We
must stop reading now and get ready for

dinner; we can read this evening." With small children it is often well to prepare them for the command in some such way as, "Five minutes more, and my little girl must put up her dollies." These, however, are mere devices used by the quick-witted mother; but Froebel would have the *law* by which the will-power is developed distinctly understood. The instinct of recognition must be comprehended in order that this law may   properly applied.

As soon as a child arrives at a perception of his own individuality this instinct awakens— he desires his individuality to be acknowledged by the people about him. The recognition usually comes through their expressed opinions concerning him and his conduct. Froebel says, in the motto to the little song called "The Five Knights,"—

" Dear Mother, use your best and your most watchful care,
    When first he listens to some stranger who is there;
    Life's truest voice has struck upon his ear,
    A new life-stage begins, but do not fear."

The " new life-stage " refers to the dawning realization in the child's mind that he "lives not in life alone." In the little game of " Peek-a-boo," common to all nurseries, Froebel traces the child's pleasure in the game to this joyous delight in being recognized. "It is not so

much," says he, "in the hiding of your dear
child, as it is in the joyful anticipation of being
found again by you." The instinct is as old as
the race.   We find outlined upon the walls of
the Egyptian tombs pictures of their rulers and
leaders, towering like giants above the armies
which followed them; not that they were physically larger, but these pictures were intended
to portray recognition of their superiority,
their larger individuality.   Wherever man has
had the power to accomplish the desires of his
heart we have found him building for himself
tombs and monuments, that he as an individual
might be recognized by future generations.
From what comes the love of wearing medals
and badges, but from the fact that they are the
external sign given by some society or association as a testimonial of the worthiness of the
individual to become a member of the organization?   With nations it is the same.   They
build beautiful temples, and magnificent state-
houses, and other grand and imposing build-
ings, that surrounding states or nations may
acknowledge their enterprise, wealth, and
artistic or religious superiority.   It is owing to
this instinctive desire for recognition and
approval that public opinion has so strong a
hold upon the mass of mankind.   What is

public opinion but the aggregation of the recognition of many individuals? It is not the number of people collected together which makes civilization, but the influence engendered by the thought of the community, or, in other words, the advance of public opinion. One era of time allowed the putting to death of cripples and weaklings; in our age public sentiment has made it the most sacred obligation of mankind to tenderly care for them. This atmosphere of public opinion surrounds us at all times. The hero alone rises much above it, and almost beyond redemption is the soul that sinks into entire indifference to it. In talking of this subject an old farmer once said to me, "I sometimes find a six-foot high stalk of corn in a five-foot high field, and occasionally I find a seven-foot high stalk in a six-foot high field; but I never find a seven-foot stalk in a five-foot field." It is the same thought better expressed by Emerson when he said it took four hundred years of culture and education and French salons to produce a Madame De Staël.

Drummond refers to this same subtle influence of the opinions of others. In his little book called "Modes of Sanctification," he says: "In your face you reflect your nationality. I ask a man a question, and I find out in ten seconds

10

whether he is a Northerner, a Southerner, a
Canadian, or an Englishman. He has reflected
his country in his very voice. I see reflected
in a mirror that he has read Herbert Spencer
and Huxley and Darwin; and as I go on
watching him, as he stands and talks to me, his
whole life is reflected from it. I see the kind
of state he has been living in, the companions
he has had; he cannot help reflecting, he cannot help himself from showing the environment
in which he has lived, the influences that have
played around him. As Tennyson says, 'I am
a part of all that I have met.' Every man is
influenced by the people and things that sur-
round him. You sometimes see husband and
wife, after half a century of fellowship, changed
entirely into the same image. They have gone
on reflecting one another so often that they
have become largely made up of the same
qualities and characteristics. That is the great
doctrine of influences: we become like those
with whom we associate."

The child comes into this moulding atmosphere of opinions floating about him while the
inborn instinct of recognition is within him,
reaching out eagerly for the approval of the
public opinion of his little world. Froebel
would have the mother take advantage of this

condition of things and train the instinct
aright; for, like all other instincts given to the
child, it can be trained upward or downward.
If the mere external surroundings, appearances,
or other incidentals, are what is praised or
approved, vanity is engendered. Vanity is all-
devouring, insatiable, never-satisfied, and consequently degenerates into bragging or into
an exaggeration of its merits in order that it
may obtain more praise. Bragging naturally
descends into lying and other forms of deceit.
If, however, the approval has been given to the
child's endeavor rather than his appearance, to
his motive rather than his deed, the hungering
desire for more approval leads him into greater
effort. This engenders love; and love of this
sort borders close on reverence. Thus the
mother has in her hands the powerful instruments of praise and censure. That which she
praises, the child will strive for; that which she
has unvaryingly censured, the child will avoid—
provided, of course, that she is consistent in
her adherence to the standards which she
places before him. The real standard—that is,
the standard which the life and conduct show,
not merely the standard preached—becomes the
child's ideal. Care should be taken not only in
the approving or disapproving of the people

about him, but much judgment must be exercised in what to approve of in the child himself. *Character* is to be praised rather than *clothes;* effort which helps to strengthen the character rather than any external gift or attraction whatsoever.

I knew of one mother whose child's beautiful golden curls attracted so much attention that the mother saw the effects of growing vanity and self-consciousness in the child. So great was her love for her little daughter, so clear her insight and so strong her will-power, that with her own hands she quietly cut the beautiful shining curls from off the little head. I know of but few mothers who have such courage. The sweet, unconscious beauty of character, developed at a later period in the daughter, showed the wisdom of the mother. We have in our kindergarten a little game in which one child is placed in the center with his eyes closed, and another is sent out of the circle. The first opens his eyes and tries by memory to tell the name of the missing one. One morning, when the child who had been sent to the center of the circle could not recall the name of the absent one, another little one ventured to assist his memory by saying, "She had on a green dress, and stood next to me." Instantly one of the older boys of the kindergarten, whose two years had taught him much, exclaimed with an emphatic shake of his head, "It doesn't make any difference what you wear or where you stand, it's what you can do." This was the result of my having always described the child sent from the circle when playing the game and help was needed, by some of his meritorious activities. I smiled to myself as I thought of the change in position in the world at large which such a standard set up by the emphatic boy would create. Yet, is it not the true test to which time finally brings all mortals? What in our eyes to-day is the finery in which the monarchs of the sixteenth century arrayed themselves, compared with the deeds of Luther? What is the social rank and worship which the Emperors demanded, compared to the reverence which we now give to the name of Epictetus?

Well-told stories, which have in them admirable traits of character, are powerful instruments in the hands of mothers and teachers. I remember at one time, as the Thanksgiving season approached, I decided to lead the children of whom I had charge to desire to make to a certain hospital a Thanksgiving offering of fruit saved through self-denial from their own luncheons. Realizing that effort was best

made when an ideal towards which to strive
was placed in an interesting manner before the
child, I told them a story of a little boy and
girl, taking care to make the two children in
the story as attractive as possible to their
young hearts. At the end, my little hero and
heroine decided to do without oranges for
breakfast for a week, and to send them to some
little children across the street who were less
fortunate than themselves. I then described,
as vividly as possible, the great pleasure and
delight which was experienced by the surprise
of the other children, and the satisfaction felt
by the little givers. The story ended in a
bright, lively manner, and nothing further was
said. The next day when luncheon time came,
one of my older boys said, "I am going to save
my orange to-day for some little child who
hasn't one." "So am I !" "And I !" "And
I !" exclaimed other little children. The next
day I told them of the hospital which I had
visited, and of the pleasure I thought it would
give the invalids if they knew that some dear
little children were intending to send them part
of their fruit for Thanksgiving day, and pro-
posed that those who wished to share their good
things with others should put them all together
and send them to the hospital. The suggestion

was received with delight. Voluntary offerings were given each luncheon-time from then to the day before Thanksgiving. I do not mean to claim by this that any especial influence is obtained or effect produced by the "goody-goody" stories in which supernatural children do unnatural things; but simply that the true, wholesome, generous deed, within the possibility of the child's performance, can be made so attractive in its ideal form of story or game that the child voluntarily attempts to do likewise. "The deeds attained by great souls," says Alger, "become the ideals towards which lesser souls strive." In fact, the greatest thing that a hero does for the world is to *be* a hero and thereby inspire others to heroic living. When this holding of the ever-advancing ideal before the child in so attractive a manner as to draw his affections toward it is once understood, the mother or teacher can lead the child *to will to do* almost anything.

When we see the little street Arabs of our large cities, ragged, dirty, and hungry, smoking cigarettes or cigars with a triumphant air of having attained a much-envied distinction, we know that their standard of manhood is measured by the length of the cigar or size of a pipe which a man can smoke. We know that

high ideals have never been given to their
little souls, and that they have reached out for
some standard by which to measure their
growing manliness, and have taken this external
distinction as the test. With this thought in
our minds, we cannot urge too strongly upon our
public schools the celebration of such days as
Washington's Birthday, Decoration Day, and
other days which commemorate the great heroes
of a nation. So, too, have the monuments and
statues in our parks and public squares a beneficial influence. By these means children learn
to know what are the types of character which
a nation delights to honor.

Froebel so well understood the value of
placing attractive ideals before children that he
has given us a little dramatic game of "The
Five Knights." This can be used as a little
song or play with the baby in the nursery, in
which case the fingers galloping over the table
represent the knights galloping into the court-
yard of the castle. With the older children in
the kindergarten it is usually dramatized by
five children being selected to represent the five
knights. These are sent out, and at a certain
stage of the game come galloping into the
room, always upon an imaginary charger such
as would have delighted the souls of the heroes

of old. True to his method of always choosing
the symbolical thing by which to teach the
child, Froebel has selected the knight as a
symbol of the highest public opinion. They
not only draw forth the child's admiration of
the man on horseback, with his power to
control the brute-force beneath him, but they
also symbolize that class of persons who have
the most complete control over themselves, who
were universal when the rest of the race was
feudal and narrow. Knighthood arose among
the class of men who forswore all that was low
and debasing when the world was sunk in ignorance and sensuality, and the word still remains
as a title of the best of the race. When we
speak of knightly conduct we have reference to
all that is chivalrous and truly noble. Froebel
thus gives to the mother the hint of the class
of persons to whom a child shall look for
approval or disapproval. It is the base fear of
the disapprobation of the "common herd"
which deters many a man from stepping out of
the rank-and-file and placing himself on the
side of the new and needed reform; but it is the
love of the approval of the really best people
which becomes an incentive for the most earnest
endeavor upon the part of the human soul.
Much, then, depends upon the one to whose

opinion the child listens.   The final aim of the
mother's or teacher's training is to have him
bow in complete obedience to the still, small
voice of God within him; but many rounds of
the ladder have to be patiently climbed before
this supreme strength of will can be obtained.
A regard for public opinion is but one stage of
the development of the will-power.

One day I noticed that a little girl who was
very self-willed was sewing the card given her
in an irregular and disorderly manner. "Oh,
Elizabeth," I exclaimed, "you are not doing
that right! come here and let me show you how
to do it."   "No," answered the child in a self-
satisfied tone, "Elizabeth likes it this way." I
saw that I must appeal to the public opinion of
the table of babies about her in order that I
might lead her to voluntarily undo the work.
So I asked her to show the card to the other
children.   As is usually the case, public opinion decided in the right, and the children said
they did not like it.   "But Elizabeth likes it,"
persisted the child.   "It's Elizabeth's card,
and she is going to make it this way." I saw
that the little community of her own equals had
not sufficient weight to influence her, and from
her manner I knew that it was mere caprice on
her part.   So I said, "Come with me and we

will go over to brother's table and see what
they think of it." We held the card up before
the next older children, and I said pleasantly,
"Children, what do you think of this card?"
"It is wrong," they exclaimed, "the soldiers"
(meaning the vertical lines) "are all tumbling
down." By this time the public opinion of our
little community had begun to have an effect,
and the child turned to me and exclaimed, "It
is a bad, nasty card, and Elizabeth will throw
it into the fire," starting at the same time
toward the open grate in the room. "Oh, no,
my dear," I exclaimed, "let's go over to the
table where the big children are. Perhaps
they can tell us something to do with it."
With that we walked across the room to the
table at which my older and better-trained
children were at work. After praising the
forms which they were making with their
sticks, in order to arouse within the child's
mind a still higher appreciation of their judgment, I said, "Our little Elizabeth has a card
she wants to show you and see if any of you
can tell her what to do with it." The card was
held up, somewhat unwillingly this time, and
the children without hesitation said, "She must
take out the crooked stitches and put them in
straight." The oldest boy at the table added,

"Come here, Elizabeth; I'll show you how to do it." With that her little chair was drawn up beside his larger one, and for ten minutes the two patiently worked over the tangled card. At the end of that time Elizabeth brought the card to me and in triumphant delight exclaimed, "Now everybody will say that Elizabeth's card is pretty!" I had no further trouble with the child in this particular direction of taking out work when wrongly done. This, of course, would not be the right method of dealing with a very sensitive child. The story shows the need of increasing the standard of judgment by which the child is to be measured, in proportion to the child's estimate of the worth and value of his own opinions. *The chief object in appealing to public opinion is to create a constantly advancing ideal toward which the child is attracted, and thereby to gain a constantly increasing effort on his part to realize this ideal.* The ideal is usually best seen, as said before, in the opinions expressed in the presence of the child. With this thought in mind, what think you of the mother who tells in the child's presence, with evident amusement, of the naughty tricks performed by him? Or of the father who pours into the ear of the admiring little listener, tales and anecdotes of what a bad boy he was, and the trouble and mischief which he caused; or of the friend who places in the hands of the growing boy such ideals as those portrayed with sprightliness in "Peck's Bad Boy"?

But to return to our symbolic game. The knights come galloping into the supposed court-yard and ask the mother the privilege of seeing her *good* child. They sing:

> "We wish thy precious child to see,
>   They say he is like the dove so good;
>   And like the lamb of merry, merry mood.
>   Then wilt thou kindly let us meet him,
>   That tenderly our hearts may greet him?"

The supposed mother then holds out the imaginary child to their view, and in her turn sings:

> "Now the precious child behold,
>   Well he merits love untold."

At this point the knights take up the song with the words:

> "Child, we give thee greetings rare,
>   These will sweeten many a care;
>   Worth much love the *good* child is,
>   Peace and joy are ever his;
>   Now we will no longer tarry,
>   Joy unto our homes we carry."

Here is dramatically pictured forth the knightly characters seeking and praising the *good* child,—the mother with joy and pride holding him up to their view, not because of any external condition whatsoever, but he is precious because he *merits* love. Nor is the goodness left vague and indefinite, for in the explanation at the back of the song-book the child asks the mother what was the song the knights sung as they rode away, and the mother tells him that it is a description of a good child. "Now, mother, we will listen to the song sung by the knights so gallant, gay, and strong, 'Come children quickly come, and hear the song we sing of this baby dear.'" Then follows the little song in which are distinctly brought out the characteristics of activity, perseverance, love, gratitude, and reverence, all of which are virtues which the childish heart can understand. Thus the ideal presented in this little game is made definite and distinct, and the dim feeling is aroused in the child's mind that such are the characters which the best mothers and the gallant knights admire and praise, and this ideal becomes his ideal. That these are the impressions made upon the child by such games cannot be doubted by any one who has seen this game played in a well-organized Kindergarten; but testimony is not wanting of the after-effects of such games. A little girl was in one of our

Kindergartens for two years, and was afterwards taken to Europe by her parents and remained away from Kindergarten influence for seven or eight years. Upon her return to America a friend asked her what she remembered of her Kindergarten experience. "Very little," she replied; "I have been so entirely shut away from any association with the thought of it that it has nearly passed out of my memory. Of course," she added, "I remember some things." "What," persisted the inquirer, "do you remember most distinctly?" "Well, for one thing," said she slowly, "I remember a little game we used to play in which some knights came galloping into the room. I do not remember much about the details of the game, but I can recall even now the great waves of joy which used to pass over me as we played the part of holding out the *good* child for the knights to see."

In one lovely home, where the mother had learned to comprehend the underlying thought of this little game and had explained it to the father, the latter took upon himself the role of the knight. Each evening when he came home, their little boy ran out to meet him, and the father took him up in his arms, then turned and asked the mother if Henry had tried to be

a good boy during the day. If she replied
yes, the father and son had a royal good romp
until dinner-time. If her reply was *no*, the
father quietly and solemnly set the little fellow
down upon the floor and walked out of the
room. So earnestly did the child learn to look
forward to this nightly approval or disapproval
of his conduct, that he would often stop in the
midst of his play during the day and ask his
mother if he had been good enough for her to
say *yes* that night.

In the second part of the song of "The
Five Knights," the knights again come and
greet the mother, asking to see her good child.
This time the mother sadly shakes her head
and says:

> "   friendly knights, I grieve to say,
>   I cannot bring him to you to-day;
>   He cries, is so morose and cross,
>   That all too small we find the house."

The knights then turn, and as they leave the
mother, they sing,—

> "Oh, such tidings give us pain;
>   We would have sung a joyous strain;
>   We'll ride away, we'll ride afar,
>   To where the good little children are."

In this way the child gets the idea that the
best people of the world are attracted toward

that which is good, and fly from that which is evil. In fact, we need scarcely say of the best people, is it not the virtue which is shown in each individual that causes him to be loved at all? Is it not the faults of people about us which separate us from them? The sooner the child learns the unifying effect of good, and the isolating effect of evil conduct, the more earnestly will he strive to attain unto the one and to avoid the other. Censure is as necessary as praise in making definite the ideal set before the child. Its office should be rightly understood, however. The supposed child in this song, dramatized by the real child, gives pleasure to his mother and the brave knights when he is good, and sorrow and pain when he has done wrong. Thus comes to the child the beginning of the thought, that as a man cannot live unto himself alone, so too he cannot sin unto himself alone; that every deed has its effect upon others. In the third phase of the song, the knights again come and inquire of the mother concerning her child. This time she joyously replies that her child has become so good that he is very dear to her, and that she cannot spare him to them. At this the knights wave their hands in congratulation and trot swiftly away. Here **we** have the final stage in this progressive drama, illustrating how to train the child by means of holding a beautiful and attractive ideal before him.   Joy, praise, love and comradeship are shown to have been merited by the *good* child; regret, sorrow, pain and isolation are shown to be the consequences of wrongdoing.   Return of companionship, forgiveness of his wrong-doing, and harmony, can be restored when the child turns from his wrongdoing and strives to do right.   This last point is an important one.   It cannot be too earnestly considered.   The reconciliation after the wrongdoing means much for the future nearness of the child to the one who has forgiven him.   As in this little game the knights were ready to come again with their welcome and approval as soon as the child was worthy of it, so too should the child in real life feel that it is his own wrong-doing only which separates him from those he loves.

If you must say, "You cannot come into mamma's room," always add "*until* you are more courteous."   Never forget that little word "*until;*" it means that the ideal can be restored and the child can again strive to realize it, through patient, earnest endeavor.   There must be no failure of sympathy upon your part the moment it is asked for.   In the depth of isolation caused by wrong-doing, let there be the underlying feeling upon the part of the child which prompted the prodigal son to say, " I will arise and go unto my father." This is the one hope which the despairing soul has. In every way let the child feel that it is *his wrong-doing alone* which causes the separation; that underneath *are* the everlasting arms of love. Thus will he learn the meaning of the message of Christ to the world that he came not to reconcile God unto man, but man unto God. And little by little will come the realization that *free-will is not the liberty to do whatever one likes, but the power to compel one's self to obey the laws of right*, to do what ought to be done in the very face of otherwise overwhelming impulse.

CHAPTER VIII.

THE SOUL.

THE INSTINCT OF REVERENCE, OR THE TRAINING OF THE WORSHIP.

Rightly understood, the tell-tale body proclaims every mood of the inner world. If a child comes bounding forward with outstretched arms and radiant smile, the mother knows that there is working within no conscious remembrance of wrong which needs reproof, no thought of command disobeyed. Let him answer her call with dragging step or downcast eyes, and she knows that something is wrong; that a barrier has been raised between them. In many less pronounced ways the attitude of the child's body and the expression of his face help the mother instinctively to read what is going on within her offspring's mind, even before he can tell her in words of his likes and dislikes, his desires and emotions. If all mothers knew that the soul could be read by means of the body, there would be less misunderstood childhood and fewer great and painful gaps between parent and child.

Here again we find that *insight* proves and makes strong the natural *instinct* of the mother. Here again we see that study, travel, and breadth of culture can become aids for this highest work of woman, namely, child-culture. All study of art shows that the great painters, sculptors, poets and dramatists, have depicted certain inner states of mind or soul by similar attitudes of head, hand and body. For example, the clasped hands denote entreaty. In Vedder's illustration of Omar Khayyam's Judgment Scene, the Recording Angel is seen above with his Book of Judgment, and below are seen the clasped hands of the terrified and beseeching multitude. No *faces* are needed to add to this tale of despair; the hands alone tell us the story, the whole story. Over and over again do we find this external bodily gesture made to express the internal condition of the mind.

One morning, in one of our large kindergartens, a young and somewhat inexperienced director was trying to teach the children a new song in which the fingers of one hand represented the pigeons flying in and out of the house made by the other hand. One shy little fellow did not take part in the dramatic representation. I saw from the nervous twisting and clasping of his hands that it was no willful disobedience, but shyness and dread of being made conspicuous which prevented the child from imitating the teacher's motions. Unaccustomed to reading her children by their bodily gestures, the young teacher turned to the child and said: "Freddie, why do you not show how the little birds fly?" In a moment the two tiny hands were clasped in entreaty. Still the unseeing director did not understand the appeal for mercy, but, with the best of intentions, took hold of the little fellow's fingers and began to move them for him. This was too much for the child, and he burst into a flood of tears, which astonished the poor girl who had intended only loving help, but who in reality had dragged his young soul into the very publicity from which he was pleading to escape.

The *clenched* hands denote the struggle within, and great artists often use them as the only marked sign of the inward turmoil which the calm face and strong will are determined to conceal.

The open and extended palm, which we see in so many of the pictures and statues of the saints, indicates entire freedom from deceit or concealment, as if the body as well as the lips were saying : "Purge me, O, Lord, cleanse me with hyssop that I may be clean." Just as surely do the hands of a little child tell us of his inner frankness or deceit. Does not the child oftentimes instinctively put his hands behind him or nervously twist them into the folds of his dress or apron when he is being questioned, even though a forbidden sweet is not *now* in the hidden hand? Many a mother or kindergartner in a trying moment could discover the truth or falsehood of a child by the right understanding of this unconscious language of his hands, and thus there would be avoided that sad catastrophe of unjust accusation.

In the kindergarten one morning, soon after the entrance of a new child, I asked the circle of children seated about me to show me the little finger families, that we might learn a new song about them. All the little hands were held up with palms toward me, save the one new child, who in a timid, shy manner held his palms averted. A word was sufficient to turn them into the franker position which the others had taken, but in a moment or two they were again turned away. After we had finished the exercise and the children had gone to their table for work, I said to my

assistant, " We must watch that new boy
carefully.   He has too secretive a nature."
Before noon that day, as I passed around the
table to observe and commend the clay work
of the different children, I found none upon
his board.   I asked where it was, and he made
no reply ; but the child who sat next to him
said, "He stuffed it all into his pocket."   So
soon did this secretiveness, discovered by the
position of his hands, begin to manifest itself in
the hiding of material which he did not understand was already his own.

In Leonardo di Vinci's great picture of the
Last Supper, the character of each of the disciples is plainly shown by the hands.   Even
those of Our Lord are made by this master
painter to express the two-fold nature of his
struggle.   The one hand with down-turned and
averted palm clearly says: "If it be possible,
let this cup pass from me."   The other, with
upturned and receptive palm, calmly indicates
the words, " Not my will but Thine be done."

The position of the *head* portrays the true
mood of the soul.   The rapt and devout saint
who thinks not of earth or of its attractions,
is represented with face turned skyward: the
penitent and humbled Magdalene turns her
bowed face to the earth, and most significantly

is told the story of repentance, forgiveness and redemption, by that sin-stained face turned upward towards heaven's light. To me the church of the Madeleine in Paris is truly a representative of the name it bears, in that all the light within its windowless walls comes from the skylight in the roof above: it is the upturned face expressed in the architecture as well as in the paintings on the walls. The mother or teacher who understands these things will quietly wait before disturbing a child, whose face is thoughtfully turned toward the cloud, moon, or shining star, and will not dare to break in upon the reverential mood. The attitude of the body will suggest to you whether it is an idle day-dream in which the child is indulging, or a communion of his little soul with higher things. How much may be learned from the childish head which bows before the stern reproof or searching glance! The close observer will notice that when shame *alone* is disturbing a sensitive child, the head droops; if with shame is commingled love and a desire for reconciliation, the head leans a little to one side as well as downward; if the head is bowed, but averted, the conquest is but half made, the sin is admitted but the heart is not won.

The degree to which the soul can express itself through its body varies of course with different children. To the true mother the child's eyes are too well known as the open door to his soul's condition to need more words from me. Perhaps no other part of the body speaks in such a subtle manner of the inner rightness or wrongness as the chest. It is here that the sense of courage, honor, and self-respect, or their absence, is plainly declared. What is it which has given Mr. Daniel French's study of the Minute Men at Concord the power to stir every American heart? Mildness and determination sit upon the brow and hover around the closed lips; courage and suppressed indignation are shown in the strong hands; alertness and readiness to act upon the moment are to be read in the position of the body; but the following immortal words are as plainly declared by the expanded chest as by the written historic Declaration of Independence:

" When, in the course of human events, it becomes necessary for one people to dissolve the political bands which have connected them with another, and to assume among the powers of the earth the separate and equal station to which the laws of nature and of nature's God entitle them, a decent respect for the opinions of mankind requires that they should declare the causes which impel them to the separation.

"We hold these truths to be self-evident—that all men are created equal; that they are endowed by their Creator with certain inalienable rights; that among these are life, liberty, and the pursuit of happiness."

Whoever has witnessed Edwin Booth's "Shylock" has seen the character of the sordid, self-debasing usurer almost as plainly delineated by the sunken chest as by the words of Shakespeare. Imagine, if you can, Uriah Heap with a broad, expanded chest! Of course, physical disability must not be confounded with moral unsoundness; the former shows its depressing symptoms in *all* of the moods of the child, that is, it is permanent; the latter affects him only temporarily when the sense of self-respect is at low tide.

It was my good fortune to meet once a week, for a year or more, with a band of earnest teachers of all grades. For weeks we discussed what outer sign would help us to discover whether the unfulfilled task of the child was due to a physical disability, to mental disinclination, or to mere caprice. With this thought in mind we watched and studied our pupils; the brightness or dullness of the eye was no criterion, as too often an inward fever gave an added sparkle to the eye, an added flush to the cheeks; the clearness of the skin did not denote always freshness and purity of blood, it being oftentimes a matter of inheritance. Indication after indication was suggested, discussed and tested. Finally, it was agreed that the well child carried at all times an active, expanded chest, except when a sense of shame or loss of integrity overpowered him, when the sunken chest proved the certainty of wrong conduct; also that the child whose physical state is a hindrance to his mental effort could be known by his sunken chest which never expanded. In a word, that this part of the body rarely fails as a sign by which the thoughtful, alert mother or teacher may read moral rectitude or its opposite.

Without self-respect there is no possibility of building up a law within. A human being who has it not must remain forever subject to an outside law: *noblesse oblige* must be an unknown power to him. Therefore, any marring of that precious germ is of incalculable injury to the child's future stability and strength of character. Let me give you an illustration of the value of this knowledge of attitudes to those who must deal with that sensitive and yet

important thing, a little child's self-respect.
We were playing one morning in Kindergarten
a game which requires a quick galloping on
the part of some of the children while the others remained sitting. As the horsemen came
galloping by, one little fellow stuck out his
foot in an attempt to interrupt the play; it
was his first violation of the rule of all our
games, which is *non-interference with the rights
of others;* so I smiled and shook my head;
again the horsemen came careering past, again
the little foot went out to interrupt the gallop;
this time I said: "Charlie, do not do that, it
spoils our game." A third time the horsemen
had to make their charge, and a third time the
obstinate little foot went out; this unmistak-
ably was open, conscious wrong-doing, and
must be effectually checked and at once. I
stopped the game and said: "Children, we cannot finish our play; step back to the circle;
Charlie has spoiled it for all of us." There
was the dead silence usual upon such infre-
quent occasions. All took their places in the
play circle, and all eyes were turned toward
Charlie. The little head began to sink; this
was an indication of the inward shame which I
intended he should feel, as the laws of each of
our games are precious to us all and the train-

ing into absolute obedience to these laws is one
of the best things in the Kindergarten; but at
the same time that the little head went down,
the chest began to sink, and I saw that my
reproof had been too great for the little fellow;
his self-respect had been injured. In a moment
I was on my knees beside him with my arms
around him; the few words of needed apology
were soon given by him and accepted by me,
but the chest did not come up to its natural
position until, when the play-time had ended,
I turned and asked him to lead in the march
back to the seats, thereby showing my returning respect for him.

We have been speaking of the aid which this
study gives to our understanding of the child.
Let us now turn to the value of it in helping
us to train him aright.

*The effect of the body upon the mind is not
generally appreciated.* That a sound mind
can work freely, a well-balanced character
develop fully, only in a sound body, is admitted by all; but the more subtle influence
is not so easily comprehended. Of equal
importance is this other side of the question.
If mind or soul acts upon the body, the
outward gesture and attitude also reacts upon
the inward feeling. The artists of the world

have portrayed the former; the thinkers have taught us the latter, and our close study of the child verifies them both. The soul speaks through the body, and the body in return gives its command to the soul. Try for a moment to think intently upon some difficult subject with your body in a lazy, relaxed posture, or arouse your body to a perfectly erect position, similar to the one given us in that beautiful portrait of the Queen Louise of Prussia, and see for yourself the effect which it produces upon you; you can then understand why the military position is obligatory to the soldier, the constant *attitude* of courage engenders the soldierly virtue. What is the advice of the wide-awake business man to the discouraged and faint-hearted friend who comes to him for counsel? "Hold up your head and be a man," he says, unconsciously coupling the physical attitude with the desired mental condition. Plato, in his "Republic," claims that the right training of the body in gymnastics, in time with some rhythmical music, has an undoubted effect upon character, the gymnastics tending to develop the spirited part of man's nature and the musical accompaniment toning this development down to gentleness, but not to effeminacy. He adds,

"Those who devote themselves to games *exclusively* become ruder than they ought to be."

In the second part of "Wilhelm Meister," Goethe's master-work on education, the children in the ideal Province of Pedagogy are trained to take one of three attitudes, according to their degree of development, whenever an overseer or teacher passes, whether it be in school room, playground or field. The youngest fold their arms crosswise on the breast and look cheerfully towards the sky; the intermediate ones have their arms behind them and look smilingly upon the ground; the oldest ones stand erect boldly, with arms at the side, turning their heads to the right and placing themselves in a row instead of remaining alone like the others. Naturally enough, Wilhelm Meister inquired as to the supposed effect of these strange postures upon the children. "Well-bred children," replied "The Three," "possess a great deal. Nature has given to each everything which he needs of home and abundance. Our duty is to develop this. Often it is better developed by itself, but *one* thing no one brings into the world, and yet it is that upon which depends everything through which a man becomes manly on every side.

If you can find it out for yourself, speak out."
Wilhelm bethought himself for a short time,
and then shook his head. After a suitable
pause, they exclaimed, "Veneration!" Wilhelm was startled. "Veneration," they repeated,
"it is wanting in all, perhaps in yourself.
You have seen three kinds of gestures: we
teach the three-fold veneration. The three
combine to form a whole, then widen into the
highest power and effort. The first is reverence for that which is above us; the arms
folded on the breast, the cheerful glance toward
the sky. That is precisely what we prescribe
in our untutored children, at the same time
requiring witness of them that there is a God
above who reflects and reveals himself in our
parents, tutors, and superiors. Second, veneration for that which is below us; the hands
folded on the back as if tied together, the
lowered smiling glance bespeaks that we have
to regard the earth well and cheerfully. It
gives us the opportunity to maintain ourselves,
it affords unspeakable joys and it brings
desperate sufferings. If one hurts oneself,
whether intentionally or accidentally, if
earthly chance does one any harm, let that be
well with all, for such dangers accompany us
all our life long, but from this condition we

12

deliver a pupil as soon as possible.   Directly
we are convinced that the teachings of this
subject have made a sufficient impression upon
him, then we bid him be a man, look to his
companions and guide himself with reference
to them.   Now he stands erect, when in union
with his colleagues, does he present a front to
the world."   And in further conversation this
wonderful "Three" explained to Wilhelm
Meister that the three-fold gestures are to
impress the youth with the three-fold reverence, and lead to the comprehension of the
three great stages of religion, namely: First,
the heathen or ethical religion; second, the
philosophical religion, which is based upon
man's recognition of the worships of the rest
of the universe; and finally the third, or
Christian religion, which recognizes the Divine
even in humility and poverty, scorn and contempt, shame and misery, suffering and death."
This, coming from one of the world's most
acute observers and deepest thinkers, is a
strong verification of the statement before
made.

Froebel, the Apostle of Childhood, makes
use of the same thought in his "Mutter und
Koselieder," when he would help the mother
to develop aright the sense of reverence in her

child. He knew well that to develop a spirit of reverence was to develop a capacity for religion. In a talk with the mother about the little song called "Brothers and Sisters," wherein the baby is taught to slowly and softly fold his little hands together, as if the little fingers were so many children being soothed to sleep, Froebel says, "The care of the life of a child's inner and higher feeling, disposition and ideas belongs certainly to the most delicate and yet the most important and difficult part of his nature. From it springs all and develops all that is highest and noblest in the life of the individual and the race, and ultimately all religious life which is at one with God in disposition, thought and deed."

"When and where does it begin?" he asks. Then adds, "It is with it as with the germs of plants and seeds in the spring; they are there long before they are outwardly visible. So we know not when and where this development commences in the human being. If we begin cultivating it too soon, we make the same mistake as by exposing seeds too soon and too much to the developing sunlight and nourishing dampness. Both would injure the tender germ. If we begin too late or too feebly, we are met by the same result; what is to be done then? How does this inner religious life show itself?"

The disease which is fastening itself upon the Christians of to-day is *self*-activity, the too great emphasis of what we must do, too little of what *God has done*. The bustling Sunday-school superintendent ; the hurried, impatient mother teaching her child his catechism while tying his necktie for Sunday-school, are but modern versions of the story of Tantalus, trying to satisfy infinite longings with finite activities. Much of the well intended primary Sunday-school work loses half of its efficiency from the teacher's not understanding that the child must be in gentle, reverential mood before he can be in the right religious attitude. The teacher should approach this holiest temple of God with reverence. Is there a place holier than the soul of a child? "You," said Froebel, "must keep holy the being of the little child. Protect it from every rough and rude impression, every touch of the vulgar; a touch, a look, a sound, is often sufficient to inflict savage wounds. A child's soul is often more tender and vulnerable than the finest or tenderest plant." Surely this is an important question for the mother who considers the training of the divine element in her child as her highest and holiest work in life. Froebel then goes on to say that there must be some necessary connection between the outside bodily gesture and the inward soul-attitude. " That so slight a thing as the gentle folding of the hands, with an external quietness, impresses the little soul with an inner feeling of collected force or unity, which is the germ of that great and strong religious conviction which leads us to speak of God as the ' Life in whom we live and move and have our being.' " He tells the mother that *by the good things which she thinks*, she can bind her child to good by many links; in other words, that the good thoughts within *her* heart tell themselves unconsciously through her bodily gestures and expressions of face, impressing silently the *child's* heart.

This is the same thought which he again expresses when he says, " The child's first ideas of prayer come to him when an infant by the mother's kneeling beside his crib in silent prayer; her bowed head and kneeling body tell of submission to and reverence for a power greater than herself; her tone of voice when she speaks of sacred things is far more effectual with the little listener than the words she says. Soft, low, sacred music, some beautiful picture of a sad-faced Madonna-like mother watching over her sleeping child, flood his little soul with reverence." It is this *sense* of reverence which he needs more than dogmatic or specific *teaching* at this early period of life. Oh, mother! Does not the thought that your real inner life inevitably tells upon that of your child, rouse in you the desire to live the highest, noblest spiritual life of which you are capable?

CHAPTER IX.

THE INSTINCT OF IMITATION, OR THE TRAINING OF THE FAITH.

The instinct of imitation is one of the most important factors in a child's education. This instinct is universal, although the power to imitate varies with different children. By universal instinct is meant one which manifests itself in all races and conditions, and not one which is the result of some peculiarity of inheritance or environment in any one class.

Imitation is the unconscious effort of a child to understand life, by doing as the people about him are doing. It is his natural impulse to test the actions of people about him. The value which the world places upon this line of conduct is shown by the adage, "Put yourself in his place," which is often used when an appeal is made for charity of judgment or even for justice. It is only when we ourselves imitate any line of work that we get into real sympathy with other workers in the same direction. "It takes a hero," says Lessing, "to write the biography of a hero;" only a man of equal or greater power can rightly

understand the hero.   Christ applied this test
when He told His disciples that they could
know the will of His father in heaven by doing
it.   We shall find that this instinct is used as
an aid in human affairs, from the teaching of
the tiny babe to wave his hand, "By-by," on
through all intermediate efforts of mankind, to
that class which takes as its ideal the highest
injunction given to man, "Be ye therefore perfect, even as your Father which is in Heaven
is perfect."

We see the manifestation of this inborn impulse in children of all stages of growth.   The
child of two years is filled with delight when
his mother teaches him to say "Bow-wow" like
the dog, or "Moo-moo" like the cow, or shows
him how to swing his ball like a bell, or to
make it spring like a cat.   The girl of the same
age, or a little older; will nurse her doll and tenderly sing it to sleep, or shake it and scold it,
according to the treatment she has seen given
to children by mother or nurse.   Often in my
twilight walks I have seen the various activities of a great city mirrored in the imitative
play of the street children.   Here is a mere
speck of humanity, toddling along with a di-
lapidated toy wagon with stray bits of wood in
it, and calling in a high childish treble some

indistinguishable words which an older sister explains as intended for, "Kindling for sale." There, rushing up the street, comes a boyish form, with arms swinging, and voice shouting rapidly, "Lang, lang, lang, lang!" and the imaginary fire-engine has flashed by. Again, if it be near election time one may meet a flaring torch-light procession consisting perhaps of but three small boys; the torch-lights may be an old broom, a picket from a fence, and a crooked stick, still the commanding spirit is there, usually imitating a drum major, and the loyal legions are marching close behind him as if inspired by the strongest party feeling. In yonder vacant lot a handful of boys are stirring up the feeble blaze of a bonfire, zealously adding to the flame such stray fagots and shingles as the neighborhood affords; listen to their talk, and you will perceive that some embryo Daniel Boone among them is carrying out his day-dream, and has led his comrades into the hardships of pioneer life in as exact an imitation of the hero of some tale as he can attain unto. The real or ideal world in which these children's thoughts live is going on in mimic representation of the older and fuller life around them. Sad is the story which the student of childhood reads in the tell-tale play

of children in the poorer districts. There is
the drunkard who is unwillingly reeling home,
escorted by a would-be policeman; here is the
daring robber who can outrun or outwit the
pursuing officers of justice, for which over-
reaching of the law he receives the vociferous
applause of his companions. A five o'clock
morning walk in one district showed me three
wrecks of womanhood standing with dejected
lassitude, waiting for the low groggeries to
open their doors to them. An evening ramble
over the same ground presented a score of ragged little girls playing with zest the part of
scolding and threatening mothers, belaboring
their children, who in turn squirmed and
twisted, cried and begged for mercy. A mother
needs but to watch the unguarded play of her
own nursery to see copied the gracious manner
of some visitor, the sincere welcome from the
kindly hostess, the wise remark of the school-
teacher, the courtesy bestowed upon the milk-
man or grocer's boy, or oftentimes the opposite
of all this—the affectation of the visitor, the in-
sincere welcome of the unwilling hostess, the
petulant reproof of the irritated school-teacher,
the lack of courtesy to the tradesman. The
child is but learning the life about him, and

by imitating it he comes into close sympathy with it.

The kindergarten games are based upon this instinct of imitation and its reaction upon character. In the game called "Bird's Nest," two children act the part of father-bird and mother-bird, and others take the part of birdlings in the nest. The former prepare the nest and feed the baby birds, and finally teach them how to fly. I think no one could witness this game and not feel that the parental love was being surely and rightly trained, and that no amount of word explanation could give the child as sympathetic an understanding of the relationship between parent and offspring as is established by such simple imitative play. We have another game in which several children, each with his hands upon the hips of the child in front of him, creep along the floor, in imitation of a worm, until finally they curl themselves up into a cocoon which lies quite still upon the floor, while the rest of the children sing "Good-bye, till you come out a butterfly." Then comes a pause in which there is sometimes represented rain or wind, or other phases of the weather, through which the cocoon remains undisturbed. When the song takes up the words, "Oh, there it is! Oh, see it fly, a

lovely, lovely butterfly," the head child creeps
out and on light tiptoe, with arms waving in the
air, flits about the room in imitation of a butterfly.   A morning or two after the introduc-
tion of this game into my Kindergarten, a
child full of life and animal spirits came running to meet me with a face which proclaimed
some good news that he was eager to tell.   He
began, "I saw a truly little worm this morning."   "Did you? Did you watch him crawl?"
"Yes, and I picked him up and put him over
into a yard, so he wouldn't get stepped on,
cause I knowed what a nice butterfly he might
be some day!"   All the glow of intense and
tender sympathy was in his face and voice; he
was indeed at one with God's creation; the
worm and he had become brothers, through his
having imitated its form of activity.   As I
looked down into his soul-lit eyes, I wondered
if this childish sympathy would not some day
help him to save, for the sake of the glorious
possibilities which lie in each of them, the little worms of humanity which crawl about the
streets and gutters of our large cities.   In another game, in which one or two of the children imitate scissor-grinders, and the others
the owners of the scissors and knives that need
repairing, we are accustomed not only to play

that we pay the household benefactors, but usually thank them quite courteously for their services. At one time I called in a real scissors-grinder, and had him sharpen and tighten some scissors, in order that the children might see the operation and the more perfectly imitate it. After he had completed his work, I paid him his money and opened the door for him to go out, when one little girl exclaimed in astonishment, "Why, you forgot to *thank him*, too!" She had in play been a scissors-grinder, and knew that recognition was due as well as money.

The parts enacted in all games of the Kindergarten are of an ennobling kind. The attraction which the role of the wild and reckless robber, who places himself outside the pale of the law, has for the child, is changed in the Kindergarten to a higher phase of the same daring spirit—for example, that of the brave and self-controlling knight, who is above law. All that is beautiful in nature—birds, bees, flowers, running water, fishes, even the stars themselves—is personified by the children; all that is useful or noble among the activities of man—the farmer, the miller, the baker, the cobbler, the cooper, the grimy blacksmith or the lordly mayor of a city—is reproduced in childish play in the Kindergarten. The children's hearts are put into harmony with all that exists, save wrong alone. One year my own study was concentrated upon Homer, and, as is natural with the true Kindergartner, that which delighted me was made into childish story and given again to my children. We had stories of the young Achilles, who, though so strong and brave, could yet control his temper, and at the bidding of the goddess Pallas Athene could put up his sword and leave the angry Agamemnon. Thrilled and enraptured, the children listened to the story of the tender and true Hector, who could put aside his baby boy and leave his wife that he might go and defend his country. With an interest akin to that of the child-race to whom the story was first sung, they listened to the wise Ulysses and his plans for capture of the Trojan city and the rescue of beautiful Helen; truly were our days heroic, proving to me that all really high and great literature holds that which is wholesome and good for the little child, when one knows how to give it aright. Truth is always helpful if wisely given. Great books live through centuries of time because of their authors' insight into truth.

Over and over again did my children ask for

the stories of those old Greek heroes. At last a child said, "Let's play Troy!" "How can we?" said I. "Oh, don't you see?" was the ready answer. "The chairs can be the walls of Troy, just so," (arranging them in a circle, backs turned outward,) "this table with four legs can be the horse, ever so many of us can get in under it and be the Greek soldiers while the rest can push us into the city, then we can get the beautiful Helen and take her home." So eager were all to attempt the dramatizing of the stories told, that chairs and tables were soon arranged, and the various names of the heroes to be represented were selected. One chose to be the strong Achilles, another the good Diomed, whom the gods helped in the fight; another was Ajax, the brave; another was Hector, and so on, until all the more heroic characters were chosen. The beautiful Helen was to be represented by a dear little fair-haired girl of four, a favorite of all. To test them I said: "Where is Prince Paris? Who will be Prince Paris?" There was a dead silence; then one boy of six, in scornful astonishment exclaimed: "Why, nobody wants to be *him*—he was a bad, selfish man!" "Well," said I, "the tongs can be Paris," and from that time forward when-

ever they cared to play their improvisation of
the old Greek poem the royal Helen was gravely
led into the walled city of Troy, with the tongs
keeping step at her side, as a fit representation of the inner ugliness of weak and profligate young princes.   I merely relate this incident to show that when children have been led
to represent the good and true, they do not
wish to play a baser part.   I firmly believe the
school of the future will see the noisy, boisterous, lawless "recess" of the primary depart-
ments replaced by lively, active impersona-
tions of historic scenes, or of the early life of
our own country, which the children are beginning to learn.   Playing these heroic parts
strengthens the heroic element within, and aids
in the building of that inner wall without
which no child is safe.

That a mother may know how she can
rightly begin the religious as well as the secular training of her child, Froebel uses the
following incident, which is an example of this
instinct of imitation: A child is taken out for
an airing on a windy day, and notices, as he
naturally would by the law of recognition, the
moving objects about him; among them a
weathervane, a very common object in Germany.   He sees that it moves from side to

side, and instinctively imitates it so that he
may understand it. The mother, whose insight tells her that this is a critical moment in
the child's life, playfully aids him in his attempt to turn his hand upon his wrist as the
weathervane turns upon the rod, and sings
some such ditty as this:

> " As the cock upon the tower
> Turns in wind and storm and shower,
> So my baby's hand is bending,
> And his pleasure has no ending."

To show the deep meaning which lies in
childish play, Froebel has used an incident of
common everyday life for each song in his
"Mutter und Koselieder," carefully choosing
those which are the most helpful to the mother. The earnest student will find imbedded
in each incident a lesson for the child which
may be eternal in its influence upon him. Thus,
in this seemingly insignificant attempt to imitate the weathervane, Froebel, with his proph-
et's eye, sees that the child is attempting to
find the *invisible* cause back of the *visible* moving object; sees, too, that it is the mother's
opportunity to begin to impress upon him the
great lesson that behind all visible manifestations of life is a great Invisible Power. Science may call it *Force*; Art may call it *Harmony;* Philosophy may call it *World Order;*

13

various religions have called it *God*, but Christianity calls it *"Our Father."* This is an important moment in a child's life, this first groping after the unseen. Are not the great, the powerful, the lasting things of life all invisible? To again turn to nature for illustrations, the great attractive and repulsive forces have thrown up the vast mountain ranges and cleft them in twain; *gravitation* has settled their crumbling fragments into level plains, and caused the water-courses to sweep in given directions; *capillary attraction* has drawn the water up into the seed cells and caused plant life to germinate and vegetation to cover the plains; *chemical action* and *assimilation* have changed vegetable and animal food into human blood; *appetites* have caused the human being to seek food and shelter and the opportunity to propagate his kind; *parental instinct* has given rise to family life; *public sentiment* has maintained the sanctity of the marriage tie and the safety of family possessions; *business credit* has made trade life possible; *patriotism* has banded these communities of civic life into national life: *religion* is yet to unify the nations of the earth into one common brotherhood. All these are invisible forces. What is the tribute paid to character,

over and above wealth and beauty, but a tribute to the unseen? Without friendship, sympathy, love, aspiration, ideality, what would
life be worth? No wonder that he who lives
only in the visible, tangible things of this
world asks the question: "Is life worth living?"
Fill a soul with the realization of the invisible, and the question needs no answer; that
soul *knows* that life is worth living. Why
are the battles with doubt, the struggles with
death, the agonies of disgrace, so awful, so
terrible, so soul-wrecking? Is it not that the
visible side of life has gained an undue foot-
hold in the sufferer's mind? Fill a life with
noble deeds, with the joy that arises from unselfish activity, and the scales will re-adjust
themselves, the "light afflictions will be seen
to work out a far more and exceeding weight
of glory."

Froebel, believing, as he himself expresses
it, that "these first impressions are the root
fibres of the child's understanding which is
developed later," calls the mother's attention
to this early interest in moving things mani-
fested by the child, and tells her that by aid-
ing his attempt to imitate the movements of
external objects, like the weathervane, she
helps him to understand them, and to know

that as an unseen force in him turns his hand so an unseen force must turn the attractive weathervane. This knowledge Froebel would have her aid by word and song; for long before a baby can distinguish words, much less understand them, he gains impressions of his mother's meaning by repeated association of word and act. That the little thinker does see that like effects are produced by like causes, is evident to anyone who has made a study of children. The lisping two-year-old baby in the family of a friend of mine was taught by the older children to solemnly bow his head up and down several times to each person present, when he was brought into the breakfast room, and to attempt to say: "How do you do?" with each ceremonious bending of the little head. The effect was absurdly droll to the other children, who with like solemnity would slowly and repeatedly return the salutation. One breezy morning he chanced to be left alone upon the veranda. The branches of the maple tree in front of the house were slowly swaying up and down, and soon attracted his attention. With puzzled interest he watched them for a short time; then a light broke over his face, and he began to bow his head in like manner, and to say "How-do! How-do!" He had logically and to his satisfaction solved the mystery ; the outside world was giving him a morning greeting. Another friend was walking along a street in a city with her child of three years. As they approached a railway crossing, an engine passed. "Mamma, " said the child, "what makes the engine go so fast?" The mother explained, as well as she could, that it was the steam inside of it which caused its rapid motion, and asked him if he did not see the clouds of white steam coming out of the top of the smoke-stack. After walking a block or two farther, a girl ran swiftly across the street; the little investigator looked up questioningly into the mother's face, and said, "Mamma, I didn't see no white steam coming out of the little girl's head,"— inferring that if steam caused one thing to pass rapidly across his path, it must cause another *like* rapid motion. That children's minds attempt to work logically, needs no other proof than to watch their grammatical errors, two-thirds of which are attempts to make their native tongue logical.

In the childhood of the world, when men tried to express their ideas of God, the first characteristic recognized and represented was *power*. So, too, we see that the child's first recognition of the unseen is ordinarily the

force of the wind. With what delight do all
children, when out on a windy day, test this
manifestation! "See!" exclaimed a little child,
"the wind can make everything do as it likes.
Where does it come from?" Each mother has
had like questions eagerly put to her. "Mamma,
what makes the smoke go up?" "Mamma, what
makes the trees grow?" Thoughtful, indeed,
should be the answer given, for it is the
searching of the young soul after the unseen
power. Then is the mother's best opportunity
for developing a reverence for the Great Unseen, bearing in mind always that increased
reverence is *increased capacity for religion.*
So great and manifold are the opportunities
afforded by nature for such lessons, that the
home and the kindergarten should bring as
much of the outdoor life as they can to the
town-imprisoned child. Right education, in
the largest sense of the word, cannot go on unless that great teacher, Dame Nature, is em-
ployed with her gloriously illuminated text-
books of field and forest, of sea and sky. From
her the child should learn its cradle-hymn of
whispering breeze, its nursery-song of running brooks, its childhood's chant from throat
of bird and hum of bees, in order that maturer
life may catch the grander, fuller harmonies,

which can come only to well-developed, reverent natures, who are ready to worship God in truth. The study of history shows us that the battle is not always to the strong, nor the race unto the swift. In olden times the forms of gods and goddesses were seen to fight first upon this side and then upon that. Old Homer tells us that "The shout of Juno filled the Greeks with courage, and caused dismay to spread throughout the Trojan ranks." Through all history an invisible power has been felt, working for victory or defeat, until in our own times a Frederick Douglass could exclaim: "*One with God is a majority!*" We scarcely need to turn to Scripture, the climax of whose revelation is summed up in these words: "God is a spirit, and they that worship him must worship him in spirit and in truth."

In speaking of social contact with others, Froebel says: "There is something else which early awakens in your child a respect for goodness, and a feeling of emulation and aspiration to attain unto goodness,—that is to say, to *be* good. These feelings are aroused in him, not by the respect and acknowledgment which you show to goodness in the *abstract*, but by the amount which you show to goodness in *others around you;* every sign of re-

spect shown to others, which appears to the
child just and merited, and above all attainable
by effort, spurs him on by awakening a generous emulation." The standard of character
which the child will strive to attain to will be
that of the people whom he meets in his home.
Let the child see that in dress it is the suita-
bility, both as to occasion and size of
purse, rather than the beauty or richness of
material, which is to be emphasized. In gifts,
let it be the pleasure given, instead of the
price of the present, which is mentioned. In
charities, let it be the *childish effort* to do and
to give, rather than any sum of money given
by the parent in the child's name. In school
work, let it be the effort put forth and the real
mastery of the point in hand, rather than the
per cent. gained, which is praised. In science-
lessons with a little child, such books as Hook-
er's "Child's Book of Nature" are of inestima-
ble value. Not only are the facts told, but that
wonderful side of science which is beyond all
explanation is always present. In story-tell-
ing, avoid moralizing, but emphasize the invisible power instead of the visible manifestation. Let me illustrate with a story, always a
favorite in my own kindergarten:

Once upon a time, in the middle of a small

village, by the side of the great ocean, there stood a little stone church; on the top of the church stood a tall spire; on the top of the spire stood a gilded weathervane. Most of the men of the village earned a living for themselves and their wives and little ones by going out in sail-boats to the deep waters of the sea, and catching fish, which they took to a neighboring city and sold for money. Each morning these fishermen would come out of their huts, and, shading their eyes from the bright sun, would look up at the gilded weathervane on the tall steeple of the little stone church. If it turned towards the sea, they knew that the wind was favorable and would fill their sails, and would help them to get out to the deep water where there was good fishing. If, however, the weathervane turned towards the land, they knew that the mighty wind was blowing away from the ocean, and that it would be useless to try to get out that day. So they would turn their boats upside down and stop up the leaks which had begun to let in the water, or they would otherwise occupy themselves on land until the wind changed. The little gilded weathervane noticed that each day the fishermen looked up to him to see whether he pointed out to the sea or in towards the land, and that they seemed to obey his slightest direction; so he began to feel that he was the most important thing in the village. Therefore, one night when the great wind came rushing down from the high mountain-tops and over the hills and plains, and reached the little weathervane, it said, in a deep, strong whisper, "Turn, turn to the sea." "No," said the little weathervane, "I am not going to mind you any longer. I am the most important thing in this village; why should I mind you? I shall turn which way I please." The great strong wind blew stronger still ; there came a cracking, snapping noise, and in a moment more the little gilded weathervane was lying broken on the ground below, and the mighty wind had swept far out on the ocean. The next morning when the fishermen came out, they looked as usual to the top of the church spire; but the little weathervane was gone. So then they looked at the boughs of the trees, and saw that they were all pointing towards the deep waters of the ocean. Then they got into their boats and went off to fish, and the foolish weathervane was left unnoticed on the ground."

As we never leave a story with a sad ending, because the effect upon the child is unwholesome, we usually add that the sexton came along by and by, and picked up the little weathervane, mended it as best he could, and after a few days put it on the top of the steeple again, and that forever after the gilded weathervane was very glad to be of use by showing the fishermen which way the great wind was blowing. Here the story ends. No moral is pointed out. The invisible soul within such stories, which has caused them to be handed down from generation to generation, will speak of itself to the child in the exact degree that he is ready to comprehend it, and will make him feel that the great invisible cause is more than any special manifestation, no matter how prom· inent. In a dim way at first, it will show him that the importance of any life comes not from its *prominence*, but from its *usefulness*. Such truths are life's great lessons, and it lies in our power to give them to the child.

The problem before every earnest mother is how to so train her child that the unseen things in life shall be as real to him as the seen. First of all she must fill *herself* with this truth, must be satisfied with no line of study or of thought which deals simply with the external facts. If she is studying history, it must be to her not a mere compilation of dates, of kings and conquests. "Of what significance to me,"

exclaimed Carlyle, " are the births, marriages
and deaths of a few petty mortals who chanced
to be called kings and queens!" And truly,
what *is* the significance, unless we seek to see
the slow dawn of freedom in the rise and fall
of nations,—a spiritual gain in the struggling
steps of the race forward? Is literature to be
studied for the sake of the beauty of style of
this writer, or of the polished diction of that
one? Why have the great books of the world
lived, while thousands of rival productions have
sunk into oblivion? Has it not been because
giant brains have lived and labored amidst
their puny contemporaries, striving to portray
Truth so that the dark labyrinth of life might
seem less dark to some poor soul? Why is
Homer still the world's great poet? Not from
beauty of expression, not from tenderness of
thought, not from power of imagery. Many
have equaled and surpassed him in these respects; but who has given to us, so powerfully
as he, the great Soul struggling against the
restrictions of authority? Who has so well
portrayed the pitifulness of uselessness, of all
great Achilles sulking in their tents, even if
their own followers are around them, when
greater and more universal causes are calling
them? Mighty indeed are the lessons which

the old bard has taught us. So it is with every other great book; it is not its form but its *soul* which has made it immortal. It is not the establishment of the Roman Catholic doctrine of hell, purgatory, and paradise; not the fierce punishment of his enemies, not even his fiery imagery, which has made Dante the shrine at which great hearts still worship. It is rather the awfulness of sin, the mighty struggle out of sin, the glory of the redeemed, pictured with such grandeur and majesty that the human soul which has approached the magnificent temple of the *Divine Comedy* feels that it has renewed its own dignity and worth. Why is it that a Carlyle cries out to the souls struggling in the hell of materialism, " Close thy Byron, open thy Goethe "? Has Goethe the literary polish and beauty of style of Lord Byron? Is it not that his strange and unsurpassed crea-tion of a Faust has proclaimed that all the cult-ure and erudition, all indulgence, all activities, cannot make life desirable until the great secret of living for others has been discovered? How much grander and more helpful becomes mythology when we cease to study it as a source of certain facts which every cultivated person should know, and begin to realize that it is the far-off voice of nations calling after

God! Of what use are the stories of the labors of Hercules, of the wings of Mercury, of the transforming powers of Circe, or a hundred other tales of a childish race, save that we see portrayed in them the dim feeling of the human heart that man must become the master of creation, must control the forces of nature and make them serve him, must be able to transfer himself with little hindrance from place to place,—aye, must govern his appetites or become beastly; in a word, that the God-element must conquer all the material outer world! Such truths are of value, though put by the child-race in such crude form; they are the *more* serviceable to the mother from the fact that they are expressed in simple, mythical shape, as the child-mind is better able to grasp truth in its poetic than in its abstract form. With thorough preparation within herself, any mother will naturally and almost without effort lead her child to value what she has learned to value.   Mothers who are deprived of the general culture which books bring, can yet keep alive in their hearts the intense realization of the all-importance of the unseen side of life; they can seek *real* people for their friends. Over and above all other avenues of inspiration they can keep their religion far beyond its

mere external, visible side. They can make
it the sweet and holy impulse from within
which shall control the inmost thought as well
as the outmost act. They can make their lives
such that religion is to them not the *mere* going to church, the reading of the Bible, the
performance of any religious duty, but *that
nearness to God* which renders all these things
a *joy.* Not until the mother has reached this
state is she ready to lead her child beyond the
petty temporal things of life, into a realization
of the great and everlasting things. Truly her
office is priestly, and great is the reward—the
greatest on earth. "A life gift" Froebel calls
this work of hers for her child; and well may it
be so called. Let her once teach him to see
the difference between the great and little
things of life, and she has placed him where
no outside storms can trouble his serenity,
where no sickness nor poverty nor lack of success nor lack of popularity can give him one
inward pang. He is master of his own life.
The petty aims of shallow people do not di-
vert him from his great purpose, and the world
exclaims, "*Truly a great soul ! Let us draw
near and gain strength from it !*"

Does any mother-heart crave more recom-
pense than this?